DAMBUSTERS

Operation *Chastise* 1943

DOUGLAS C. DILDY

First published in Great Britain in 2010 by Osprey Publishing,
Midland House, West Way, Botley, Oxford, OX2 0PH, UK
44–02 23rd St, Suite 219, Long Island City, NY 11101, USA

E-mail: info@ospreypublishing.com

© 2010 Osprey Publishing Ltd.

A CIP catalog record for this book is available from the British Library

ISBN: 978 1 84603 934 8
E-book ISBN: 978 1 84603 935 5

Page layout by Bounford.com, Cambridge, UK
Index by David Worthington
Typeset in Sabon
Maps by Bounford.com, Cambridge, UK
3D BEVs by Alan Gilliland
Originated by PPS Grasmere Ltd, Leeds, UK
Printed in China through Worldprint

10 11 12 13 14   10 9 8 7 6 5 4 3 2 1

Osprey Publishing is supporting the Woodland Trust, the UK's leading
woodland conservation charity, by funding the dedication of trees.

www.ospreypublishing.com

AUTHOR'S NOTE

I would like to acknowledge my gratitude for the generous support and
assistance of several key individuals. First and foremost I owe a deep debt
of thanks to my wife, Ann, whose encouragement and selfless support
have enabled me to bring this project to completion under the most
stressful of family circumstances.

I am also deeply indebted to my pilot friend Maj Rob Mignard, USAF
(Ret.), who first put me on to the notion that the Upkeep weapons
delivery profiles could not have been flown in the way they have been
so frequently described. Maj Mignard has personally flown the so-called
'agreed tactic' used at both the Möhne and Eder dams, and it was his
determinations – amply supported by aerial photographs – that
motivated the search for the correct attack profiles. The answer was
provided by aeronautical engineer (and fellow pilot and author)
Arthur G. Thorning, who published his own findings in his 1998 book
The Dambuster Who Cracked the Dam. He has allowed his findings to
be repeated here. I thank him for his generous, thorough and insightful
support for my own project. My thanks, too, go to noted historian Dr Don
Alberts for his critical review, corrections and suggestions.

As with Operation *Chastise* itself, this book project represents a
culmination of the efforts of several different individuals. These efforts
have come together to provide the most realistic and accurate
description possible. To each participant I reiterate my thanks.

CONTENTS

INTRODUCTION

'There can be no doubt that we must be prepared for long distance aerial operations against an enemy's main source of supply.'

Air Marshal Sir Hugh Trenchard, GCB, OM, GCVO, DSO, upon becoming Chief of Air Staff (second time), 31 March 1919

The 'Dams Raid' by the RAF's No 617 Squadron, during the horrific chaos and combat in the midst of World War II, remains a larger-than-life event even after almost seven decades of subsequent history. It was a tremendous technological achievement almost unparalleled in military aviation history – the synergistic culmination of innovative weapons science, imaginative and high-risk weapons delivery technique, meticulous planning, intensive training and daring execution. Its technological success – and exceptionally high level of sacrifice in achieving that – coupled with the almost immediate heavy-handed propaganda and public-relations offensive surrounding it have probably all assured Operation *Chastise* a place in history long after all other significant World War II achievements – barring perhaps the D-Day landings in Normandy – have faded into obscurity.

Consequently, the 'Dambusters Raid' of 1943 has become the subject of English lore and RAF legend – of almost Arthurian proportions. It has been written about more than any other single air operation, easily eclipsing the American 'Doolittle Raid' – which was very similar in many respects – the year before. Because of the raid's iconic status, most of the literature on *Chastise* has favoured myth, mystery and misinformation, largely parroting wartime propaganda and lavishly expounding on the militarily insignificant, rather than providing an objective assessment of the event. It is hoped that this book, by closely examining Operation *Chastise* as a military operation, will concisely tell the complete story in the most historically significant way.

To do this we must first know just what the raid was designed to achieve. A review of the original files on *Chastise*, held at the UK National Archives in Kew, England, reveals that the operation was aimed at strategic objectives on the economic, morale and political levels.

Economically the RAF hoped to interrupt the Nazi Reich's steel and armaments production – centred primarily in the heavily industrialized Ruhr Valley region – by flooding factories, damaging transport infrastructure (flooding canals and washing away bridges), and disrupting the supply of water (it was estimated that for each ton of steel produced, eight tons of water were required for cooling huge steel furnaces and thermal powerplants) and the supply of power from hydro-electric powerplants associated with the dams. It was hoped that interrupting steel production would have an immediate – if only temporary – effect on the manufacture of tanks, army and anti-aircraft artillery, and other heavy military equipment.

In terms of morale, the operation had two aims. The first was 'spreading panic among the population ... [and] lowering of enemy morale'; specifically in this case, it aimed to demoralise the workers in the steel mills and armaments factories and dissuade them from coming to work for der *Führer* and *das Vaterland*. The second aim related to the British home front. In the light of the long and disillusioning first three years of actual warfare against the Nazi regime, the lack of physical engagement with the Wehrmacht in anything but a peripheral theatre (North Africa), the huge maritime supply-line losses to the Kriegmarine's ravaging U-boats, and the depressingly high RAF aircrew losses in the rather ineffective ongoing bomber offensive, a notable success was needed. The accomplishment of such a high-profile air operation, combining the very best elements of what were seen as the British national character, would provide a morale-boost at home out of all proportion to the costs and the actual achievements of this risky raid.

The third and most hoped-for major aim – and the primary reason for the considerable amount of propaganda accompanying the operation – related to the highest levels of British government. This was the positive influence this unique military feat would have on Britain's allies. The Soviets had yet to achieve dominance on the Eastern Front and Stalin was clamouring for the Western allies (Great Britain and the USA) to open a 'second front' against the enemy. The impatient and sometimes impetuous Americans lacked confidence in British military leadership, technology, tactics and techniques, given Britain's disappointing record of misadventure in the first three years of the war. A dramatically successful high-profile aerial operation would do much to solidify the support of Britain's two main allies in pursuing the war to a victorious conclusion.

It is against these fairly concisely proscribed – if somewhat nebulously defined – objectives that Operation *Chastise* should ultimately be judged.

'Après moi, le deluge' ('after me, the deluge'). The dramatic results of a precision airstrike against what was seen as a vital strategic element of the Third Reich's heavy armaments industry: the Möhne Dam the day after 617 Sqn Lancasters attacked it with five *Upkeep* anti-dam depth charges. A little too late, that morning the Germans placed barrage balloons overhead. (UK National Archives Photo AIR 20/4367)

ORIGINS

'The time has arrived when we should make arrangements for the destruction of the Möhne Dam.'

Air Marshal Sir Charles Portal, Air Officer Commanding-in-Chief of Bomber Command, to Under-Secretary of State for Air Harold Balfour, MC, 3 July 1940

Target: the Ruhr

The Ruhr River basin developed into Germany's major industrial centre early in the modern historical period, thanks to the many nearby iron mines in the hills to the south, the availability of water (for drinking, industrial processes and transportation of heavy finished goods), the abundance of wood (as fuel for furnaces and foundries) and, later, the discovery of huge adjacent coal deposits. This combination of factors led to a burgeoning production of steel during the later 19th century that supplied armour plate and heavy guns to the Kaiser's expanding *Hochseeflotte* ('High Seas Fleet'). In the 1920s and 1930s a resurgent steel and armaments industry produced vast quantities of naval, flak and army artillery; tanks and other armoured vehicles; and petrol (gasoline) and Diesel engines powering the Führer's new mechanised Wehrmacht. In short, the Ruhr produced most of what was required to pursue Hitler's offensive strategies.

The industries of the Ruhr – of which the massive Krupp complex at Essen was the most famous – were spread across seven large cities, from Duisburg on the Rhine to Dortmund in the east, which all developed in or to the north of the Ruhr basin. To the south, rising rather abruptly some 1,250ft (400m) from the Ruhr basin and the southern reaches of the north German plain, was the Rheinisches Schiefergebirge (Rhine Massif) – a heavily wooded plateau of roughly hewn valleys and gently rolling ridges with peaks reaching to 2,750ft (840m). The mines burrowing into this great forested massif supplied the raw materials (iron and coal) for the Ruhr industries and from its folds flowed the tributaries of the two major rivers – the Ruhr and the Lenne – that supplied both water and hydro-electric power to the cities below.

Early in the 20th century two major reservoirs were created by damming two short tributaries of the Ruhr. The Möhnesee and Sorpesee directly affected the Ruhr basin. Three other reservoirs also stored water for the Ruhr basin: the Ennepestausee, on the small River Ennepe; the Hennesee, just off the Ruhr itself; and the Listerstausee on the Bigge, a tributary of the Lenne. These five dams held back a total of 254 million cubic metres of water. More than half of this water was behind the Möhne-Talsperre (Möhne Valley Dam), making the Möhne Dam the primary target.

The concentration of vital war matériel industries in the Ruhr basin naturally provided the RAF with a very attractive target for its almost Messianic vision of strategic bombing as the modern alternative to the hideous human carnage of the World War I battlefields. Anticipating the coming of World War II, in October 1937 the RAF's Director of Plans developed 16 'Western Air Plans'; the W.A.5 series of these addressed 'attacking German manufacturing resources', and subset W.A.5(b) specifically focused on bombing German industries located in the Ruhr basin. The primary targets were 26 coking plants (for steel production) and 19 coal-fired electricity powerplants (providing power to the nearby armaments factories). The RAF anticipated that it would take 3,000 bomber sorties over the course of a fortnight – with the loss of 176 aircraft – to destroy these and bring Nazi war matériel production 'to a virtual standstill'.

Reviewing the Air Staff's plan for 'knocking out' the Ruhr industries, the government's Air Targets Sub-Committee (subordinate to the Prime Minister's Committee of Imperial Defence under Sir, later Lord, Maurice Hankey) suggested that the same effect could be wrought, but without the substantial losses, by the destruction of just two vital targets, the Möhne and Sorpe dams. The committee anticipated that the effects of this would include widespread flooding, causing disruption to Ruhr production and the transport of finished goods, and the loss of water supplies and hydro-electric power needed for production processes.

The Air Ministry studied the suggestion and subsequently advised that rupturing a 'typical gravity dam' 146ft (44.5m) high and 140ft (42.7m) thick at the base was beyond the capability of current RAF ordnance. However, 'if the policy to attack dams is accepted, the committee are of the opinion that the development of a propelled piercing bomb of high capacity would be essential to ensure the requisite velocity and flight approximating to the horizontal. Even then its success is problematical.'

Thinking on similar though independent lines, in spring 1938 Bomber Command staff produced a paper entitled 'Air attacks on reservoirs and dams', which was reviewed and discussed at the Air Ministry's Bombing Committee meeting in July that year. The paper predicted that 'not only would power stations be automatically put out of action, but considerable damage would also be caused by the release of floodwater … the destruction of one dam may have the same result as the destruction of a considerable number of targets further down the chain of the industrial system'. Nevertheless, the committee acknowledged that however desirous the effect might be, the RAF lacked the means to accomplish it.

FEBRUARY 26 1943

Decision made to strike Ruhr dams with Barnes Wallis' *Upkeep* 'bouncing bomb'

Two years later – as the German panzers rampaged through France and the Royal Navy began organizing the BEF's evacuation from Dunkirk – a former member of this committee, Air Vice-Marshal (AVM) Norman Bottomley, now the Senior Air Staff Officer (SASO) at Bomber Command, suggested to his boss, Air Marshal (AM) Sir Charles Portal, that the Air Ministry be urged to develop the means to destroy the Möhne Dam. Portal was quickly convinced and forwarded a paper (authored by Bottomley) to the Under-Secretary of State for Air, Harold Balfour, arguing that the goal was 'by no means impossible [to achieve] provided the correct weapons are available'. Meanwhile, Portal proposed that the RAF form a squadron of 'at least twelve' Handley-Page Hampden twin-engine medium bombers modified as long-range torpedo carriers and stated that he desired to use them to attack the Möhne as soon as possible, 'provided the Air Ministry agreed'.

Meanwhile, on 2 May the Chief Superintendent of the RAF's Research Department directed one of his assistants, RAF Volunteer Reserve Wing Commander (Wg Cdr) C. R. Finch-Noyles, DSO, AFC, to research the means to destroy a 'gravity dam'. Responding in a paper four months later, Finch-Noyles calculated that if 20,000lb (9,072kg) of explosives were detonated 40ft (12.2m) below the crest of a dam (where the structure was about 40ft/12.2m thick) 'there seems a probability that the dam would go'.

Several practical applications were investigated. One was an air-launched missile/torpedo weighing 3,000lb (1,608kg), of which two-thirds would be high explosive, that would enter the water a half-mile from the target; it would be compass-guided and propelled by a rocket/gun device to the proper point of detonation. Another was a similar-sized, gyrostabilised, self-propelled 'hydro-plane skimmer' which upon contacting the dam's wall would fill with water and sink, detonating its explosives by hydrostatic triggers at the appropriate depth. These devices were to be delivered by a squadron of 16 Vickers Wellington twin-engine medium bombers using 'glide-bombing' approaches aimed at the centre of the dam's 'water face'. It was hoped that the repeated impacts of a series of explosions would weaken the dam's masonry to the point where the weight of water behind it forced a breach.

While the Admiralty undertook designing and experimenting with the two weapons at HMS *Vernon*, Finch-Noyles published his conclusions in a paper wordily entitled 'The high capacity short range torpedo and skimmer for conveyance by air and other craft' on 2 April 1941. The paper was sent to several individuals, including AM Sir Richard Peirse, then Air Officer Commander-in-Chief (AOC-in-C) of Bomber Command. Finch-Noyles' paper proposed that a special unit of Wellingtons be formed. The unit would develop the exact method of attack, prepare the aircraft and train the crews. Finch-Noyles stated: 'In determined hands with a singleness of purpose and freedom from disturbance, such a unit should in six months from the word "go" have effected its objects given the necessary priority.'

Peirse gave the paper to his group captain in charge of operations to examine and evaluate. On 2 June Peirse rejected the proposal, noting that previous reviews had emphasised the 'enormous quantity of explosive'

MARCH 5–6 1943

Battle of the Ruhr begins

required and saying he doubted that repeated impacts by much smaller amounts would have the desired effect.

Nevertheless, by the summer of 1941 all requisites for the future Operation *Chastise* were now firmly imprinted upon the corporate consciousness of the RAF, apart from the nature of the actual weapon to be used. There was a determination to destroy the Möhne by placing a large explosive charge against the dam wall at a sufficient depth; there was the establishment of a specific and independent Bomber Command unit tasked with doing so; and most of all there was Sir Charles Portal's interest in doing all this.

Now 'go away and play while we get on with the war'

When AM (soon to be Air Chief Marshal) Sir Arthur Travers 'Bert' Harris replaced Peirse as AOC-in-C Bomber Command on 22 February 1942, his reigning guidance from the Chief of Air Staff (CAS) – now Air Chief Marshal Portal – was: 'We should concentrate our efforts against a limited number of objectives and aim at sustaining our air attack on them. Even during the period of the short summer nights, suitable objectives are to be found in the densely populated and industrially important Ruhr area.'

However, during most of his first year in command Harris was faced with the wasteful and ineffective dissipation of effort brought about by the Battle of the Atlantic, whereby the Kriegsmarine's U-boat interdiction of Britain's maritime lifeline threatened to halt Britain's capacity to continue the war. In response, Bomber Command was directed to try to interrupt the flow of U-boats into the north Atlantic by attacking submarines in their pens at their bases on the French Bay of Biscay coast and at their construction yards in

A pre-war photograph of the Möhne Dam from RAF Intelligence files, showing all the sluices open. This photo provided some of the limited information available about the primary target, and was annotated 'Not To Be Taken Into The Air'. (UK National Archives Photo AIR 20/4367)

The Eder Dam as seen in a pre-war German postcard. As in the case of the other targets, this picture was part of the limited 'hard intel' possessed by the RAF before the raid. Note the high ground immediately behind the dam itself. (IWM Photo C 3718)

Hamburg, Germany. Thousands of tons of 500lb (226.8kg) General Purpose bombs were dropped on the bases, but did little more than scratch the surface of the pens' 16ft (3m) steel-reinforced concrete roofs.

By the start of the new year it was evident that although the RAF was indeed helping to win the Battle of the Atlantic, the major contribution was being made by Coastal Command. Harris' guidance was revised to re-emphasise the original aim and objectives of the strategic bombing campaign. This was codified following agreements reached at the first Anglo-American strategic summit meeting at Casablanca on 14–24 January 1943 (codename *Symbol*).

The resulting directive to Harris read: 'Your primary object will be the progressive destruction of the German military industrial and economic system, and the undermining of the morale of the German people to a point where their armed resistance is fatally weakened.'

Harris began the 'Battle of the Ruhr' on the night of 5–6 March, with a heavy attack on Essen – the home of the Krupp heavy armaments industry and 'the symbol of German rearmament'. First, eight De Havilland Mosquito 'pathfinder' aircraft dropped 250lb (113.4kg) target-indicator (TI) canisters, each containing 60 three-minute red pyrotechnic 'candles', purely on the basis of an OBOE (transponder-determined ranges from paired transmitters in England) intersection. Then, 22 heavy bombers dropped green TIs. Of the main force – 140 Lancasters, 141 other four-engined heavy bombers and 131 twin-engined medium bombers – 381 aircraft reported attacking the target successfully. Subsequent reconnaissance photos revealed that the centre of Essen – at the intersection of the OBOE arcs – was 'virtually destroyed' and elsewhere the 'destruction was exceptionally severe and widespread'. In fact, 53 buildings within the large Krupp complex, as well as more than

3,000 homes, were destroyed in one of the more spectacular attacks of the Battle of the Ruhr.

Essen was struck again a week later, with damage to another 15 Krupp buildings. However, a similar raid by 455 bombers against nearby Duisburg on the night of 26–27 March went awry when a large number of OBOE-delivered TIs were dropped well away from the target.

Abysmal accuracy when bombing was endemic to the RAF's night bombing programme, even when using such technical advances as GEE – a hyperbolic radio navigation aid using triangulation from three low-frequency transmitters – and OBOE. Trials conducted in broad daylight in 1938, with bombs being dropped from 10,000–15,000ft (3,048–4,572m), revealed an average 'miss distance' of 306–339ft (93.3–103.3m) – more than the length of a soccer field – depending on the type of bomber employed. Mathematically, this worked out as a 6% probability of hitting a 150sq ft (45.7sq m) object (such as a building). The estimate was reduced to a 2% probability in combat conditions.

Early on, heavy attrition on daylight bombing missions forced the RAF to switch to night bombing, and accuracy went from disappointing to appalling. The infamous Butt Report – an analysis undertaken on behalf of Prof Sir Frederick Lindemann (Lord Cherwell), Churchill's scientific advisor, by D. M. B. Butt of the War Cabinet Secretariat – analysed figures for 100 raids conducted against 28 targets on 48 nights in June–July 1941. 'Of those aircraft recorded as attacking their target … over Germany [only] one in four' got within five miles (8km) of it. The latter distance was considered close enough to the 'target area' considering that an area of 75 square miles (194sq km) approximated a city of 100,000 people. Because of the near-perpetual blanket of industrial haze over the Ruhr basin, only 10% of the bombers came within five miles (8km) of their targets, and on nights when the haze was particularly prevalent the average was 6.7%.

If British bombers could not deliver even 10% of their ordnance within five miles (8km) of target, how could they expect to hit a precise point in the centre of a dam 2,133ft (650m) wide with a single bomb heavy enough to blow a hole in masonry 40ft (12.2m) thick? Not surprisingly, when a proposal to attempt to do so was put before 'Bomber' Harris, he responded with a strongly worded negative reaction.

Although Harris failed to recognise it at the time – when briefed about it on 21 February 1943 – what he was looking at was a veritable wizard's solution.

INITIAL STRATEGY AND WEAPONS DEVELOPMENT

'The destruction of certain important dams such as the Möhne would probably do immense damage if only from the extensive flooding of industrial districts.'
Dr (later Sir) Barnes Neville Wallis, CBE, FRS, 'Note on a method of attacking the Axis powers', March 1941

As it turned out, 53-year old engineer Dr (later Sir) Barnes N. Wallis, assistant chief designer at Vickers-Armstrong (Aircraft) Ltd, had also been fascinated with solving this two-part problem, which required accurate placement of a sufficient amount of explosives.

Wallis first examined this dual problem in a 117-page study, 'Note on a method of attacking the Axis powers'. Published in early March 1941 and with about 100 copies going to various scientific, political and military 'interested parties', the study soon found its way to the small, new *ad hoc* Aerial Attack on Dams (AAD) Advisory Committee, which was under the Director of Scientific Research at the Ministry of Aircraft Production (MAP). After the director met Wallis on 10 March 1941, he asked the Air Ministry to evaluate the proposal.

The 'earthquake bomb'

Wallis had begun his study in autumn 1939 with a year-long piece of research into Germany's 'sources of supply'. Like the Air Staff, he was drawn to the Möhne Dam as one of various potentially more productive targets. Wallis dismissed the RAF's ongoing practice of 'peppering' targets with 500lb or 1,000lb (453.6kg) GP bombs as highly inefficient. By September 1940 he was convinced that a dam could only be fractured by dropping a single huge bomb – 22,400lb (10,000kg, or ten tonnes), with 15,680lb (7,000kg) consisting of high explosive – within 150ft (45.7m) of the structure at supersonic velocity so that it penetrated deep within the earth at an adjacent spot.

To obtain this velocity the 'earthquake bomb' would have to be dropped from 40,000ft (12,192m). Delivering this in turn required Wallis to design a

MARCH 17 1943

No 617 Squadron constituted

six-engine bomber, dubbed the 'Vickers Victory'. Operating above Luftwaffe fighter envelopes, with a top speed of 330mph (531km/hr), the huge unarmed bomber (weighing 107,000lb and with a 60ft/18.3m-wingspan) would have a range of 4,000 miles (6,437km) – able to reach any target under Axis control and then return.

SIR BARNES NEVILLE WALLIS, CBE, FRS, RDI, FRAES

There is a difference between being persistent and being a pest. For the first half of World War II, most senior RAF officers thought Dr Barnes Wallis was the latter.

Brilliant and eccentric, determined and arrogant, Barnes Neville Wallis started life with a lot to prove. Born on 26 September 1887 in Ripley, Derbyshire, he was the second son of four children. The family soon moved to London where his father, Charles, a general practitioner (family doctor), became crippled after contracting poliomyelitis. Wallis' mother Edith sacrificed and struggled tirelessly to provide for the children.

At the age 12 Wallis was accepted on a competitive scholarship to Christ's Hospital, a public (independent) school for the poor, where he excelled in mathematics, science and English and developed an early desire to become an engineer. He left school at 17 to begin an apprenticeship with the Thames Engineering Works, and finished his apprenticeship as a marine engineer with a shipbuilder on the Isle of Wight.

In 1913 Wallis took advantage of an opportunity to work on dirigible design and accepted a position with the aviation department of the large industrial conglomerate Vickers Ltd. There he pioneered the use of the French 'basket-weave' geodetic framework technique and in the 1920s engineered the gasbag wiring for the successful R100 airship – then the largest dirigible constructed to date.

After 1928 Wallis moved to Vickers (Aircraft) Ltd (later Vickers-Armstrong Ltd) at Weybridge, Surrey. Working for chief designer Rex K. Pierson, Wallis used his knowledge of duraluminium construction and geodetic structures to help develop two advanced, robust monoplane bombers: the Vickers Wellesley single-engine, long-range 'colonial' bomber and the Wellington twin-engine 'heavy' bomber.

Barnes Wallis was all about design efficiency – his input to the design of the R100 involved seeking the most efficient shape to allow a large airship to be pushed through a mass of air. He used the geodetic framework in the Vickers bombers because this provided the strongest structure for the least weight.

Fully aware of his high intelligence, and not blessed with the kind of personality that would keep it in perspective, Wallis regarded his intellectual inferiors with disdain. He believed that 'it is the engineers of this country who are going to win this war', while senior Air Staff officers were 'no doubt … singularly stupid'. Convinced that his own solutions were the ones to win the war, he referred to fellow British scientists working on weapons projects as 'rivals' and rarely gave credit to others. He even attempted to claim, five days before the raid, that he had invented a new rangefinder that was curiously similar to the Dann bombsight used by most of the 617 Sqn bomb-aimers in the attack.

Nevertheless, his genius prevailed when devising a successful method to destroy the 'great dams of Germany' and his persistence ensured that the solution was readily available when the RAF finally realised – and capitalised upon – its potential. While AVMs Linnell, Bottomley and Cochrane may be credited with capitalising on the solution, it is Sir Barnes Wallis who provided it.

By the time Wallis retired from Vickers in 1971, at the age of 84, he had been knighted (1968), elected a Fellow of the Royal Aeronautical Society, and awarded honorary doctorates from six major British universities. Wallis died on 30 October 1979 and was buried in Effingham, Surrey, where he and his wife Molly had spent most of their lives and raised their four children. They had also adopted the children of Molly's sister.

While Barnes Wallis pursued his 'earthquake bomb', in November 1940 the Building Research Station at Garston constructed this very precise 42ft (12.8m), 1/50th-scale model of the Möhne Dam. Over the following three months A. R. Collins used the model to test the effects of underwater explosive devices against the intended target. The model dam cracked but held. (IWM Photo C(AM) 1603)

The problem Wallis failed to address in his study was accuracy: just how could the RAF place a single bomb within 150ft (45.7m) of a structure? Additionally, devoting matériel, personnel and manufacturing resources at the level required to produce even a small force of 'stratospheric' superbombers would adversely affect the production of RAF four-engined heavy bombers. On 21 May, the service responded to Wallis: 'The Air Staff has no interest in a specialised big bomber solely designed to carry one big bomb, and your view that the single-purpose bomber offers a high probability of winning the war is not accepted.'

The 'bouncing bomb'

Undaunted, Wallis went back to the drawing board in his second-floor office in the Burhill Golf Club building at Hersham, Walton-on-Thames, and began to search for another way to achieve the same result. He spent another year on this, mostly studying the effects of explosives – in varying amounts and with different placements – against 1/10th- and 1/50th-scale models of the Möhne Dam built by the Road Research Laboratory at Harmondsworth, near London, and others near Rhayader, Wales. He then finally hit upon the solution that would confirm his genius.

As historian John Sweetman wrote in the thoroughly researched and highly detailed *The Dambusters Raid*, by this time 'he knew that American airmen had dropped bombs from low level and skipped them over the waves towards enemy ships, and he was intrigued to hear a BBC broadcast ascribe this type of attack to an RAF Coastal Command bomber in the Channel'. Curiously, Wallis' personal diaries for 1941 and 1942 are missing from the collection in the UK National Archives, so this can be neither confirmed or denied.

In an autobiographical article in 1973, Wallis described the idea almost as an epiphany: 'Early in 1942 I had the idea of a missile which, if dropped on the water at a considerable distance upstream of the dam, would reach the dam in a series of ricochets, and after impact against the crest of the dam would sink in close contact with the upstream face of the masonry.'

The critical realisation that the weapon had to be placed in contact with the dam was arrived at through A. R. Collins' continuing 'dam-blaster' experiments at the Harmondsworth laboratory in March 1942. As Wallis later wrote to Collins: 'The bouncing bomb was originated solely to meet the requirements so convincingly demonstrated by your experiments that actual contact with the masonry of the dam was essential.'

At Silvermere Lake at Byfleet, Wallis informally validated his theory by catapulting half-inch (12.7mm) wooden spheres across the water's surface. His secretary, Amy Gentry, would retrieve the 'models' using a small rowing boat. Wallis collected all his findings and revised his proposal in a paper entitled 'Spherical bomb – surface torpedo', dated 14 May 1942, which he circulated widely. Through fellow-scientist Prof P. M. S. Blackett, Wallis attracted the interest of Sir Henry Tizard, scientific advisor to the MAP, and through him acquired the use of the William Froude National Physical Laboratory at Teddington to test his hypothesis.

Conducting tests in the 640ft 'No 2 Ship Tank' on 22 days between 9 June and 22 September allowed him to demonstrate his ideas to several 'interested parties'. One of the first to witness the theory in action was Tizard himself, who three days later wrote to MAP's Director of Scientific Research, Dr D. R. Pye, saying: 'It looked very promising ... I certainly think now that a full-scale test is desirable with a Wellington.' Another visitor was AVM Sir Ralph A. Cochrane, Air Officer Commanding (AOC) 3 Group (Wellingtons). Cochrane was to become commander of 5 Group at the end of February 1943 and would be a proponent of the project, soon to be codenamed *Upkeep*.

Project *Upkeep*

An even more influential visitor was AVM Frederick Linnell, the MAP's Controller of Research and Development (CRD), who became one of Wallis' most ardent supporters. On 25 June Linnell authorised Wellington III BJ895 to be modified to carry and drop a 4.5ft (1.37m) diameter subscale mock-up sphere in ground and air tests. Even before the modifications were complete, Tizard advised 'that Wallis be instructed straight away to submit an opinion as to whether a bouncing bomb of this size [the full 7.5ft/2.3m diameter] could be fitted to a Stirling or a Lancaster'.

On 4 December 1942, Wellington BJ895 took off from RAF Warmwell with Wallis on board as 'bomb-aimer' and carrying two of the 4.5ft welded-steel test spheres. The aircraft dropped the spheres on the test range, situated in the shallow lagoon on the landward side of Chesil Beach, near Portland on the south coast of England. Both spheres burst on impact with the water. The test was repeated twice more – with the same results. Then on 23 January came a successful release: a wooden mock-up test sphere dropped at a speed of 283mph (455km/hr) and a height of 42ft (12.8m) went bounding across the water an amazing 13 times. The last of two more tests (on 5 February), using 3ft 10in. (1.17m) wooden mock-ups, achieved a range of about 1,315yd (1,202m).

Based on these tests, Wallis produced his final word on the subject: a 27-page paper entitled 'Air attack on dams' which discussed 'the effect of destroying the large barrage dams in the Ruhr Valley, together with some account of the means of doing it'. One copy was sent straightaway to Air Marshal Sir Ralph Sorley, assistant chief of the air staff heading the technical requirements division. The paper was also distributed to another 20 influential individuals over the next three months.

On 12 February, a week after receiving the paper, Sorley passed on to Linnell an appreciation of the project that stated: 'Model experiments, mathematical analysis and full-scale drops of a smaller weapon, all indicate

**MARCH 19
1943**

**Acting Wg Cdr
Guy P. Gibson
appointed
commander
of 617 Sqn**

**MARCH 24
1943**

**No 617 Sqn
activated at
RAF Scampton**

that the *Upkeep* project is technically feasible.' The very next day Sorley chaired a meeting of 13 representatives of the Air Ministry, Bomber Command, the Admiralty (who left shortly after their proposed use of conventional naval mines against the Möhne was rejected) and MAP 'to discuss the development and possible operational use of the spherical bomb'. The consensus was that MAP should continue developing *Upkeep* and that Bomber Command should be brought fully into it. It was proposed that one squadron of Lancasters be detailed for 'two to three weeks' of training and employment in May or June.

However, when briefed the next day the AOC-in-C Bomber Command, ACM Harris, vehemently objected to the scheme. He wrote: 'This is tripe of the wildest description. There are so many ifs & buts that there is not the smallest chance of it working … At all costs stop them putting aside Lancasters & reducing our bombing effort on this wild goose chase.'

Sorley's *ad hoc* committee had seen Wallis' film of the final trials with the mock-up near Chesil Beach. On 15 February – despite Harris' objections – the committee decided to produce a single full-scale example of the *Upkeep* weapon and modify a single Lancaster for operational trials. It informed the Chief of Staff, ACM Portal, accordingly. Upon learning of this, Harris immediately sent a personal handwritten letter to his boss detailing his criticism of Wallis' proposal and pleading 'I hope you will do your utmost to keep these mistaken enthusiasts within the bounds of reason and certainly to prevent them setting aside any number of our precious Lancasters for immediate modification.'

Portal also saw Wallis' film of the Chesil Beach trials at a special showing at Vickers House in London on 19 February. Unmoved at Harris' protests, he amended the *ad hoc* committee's recommendation to include modifying three Lancasters to support *Upkeep*'s development. The CAS's decision was implemented one week later when AVM Linnell convened a meeting of representatives from the Air Ministry, MAP, A. V. Roe & Co. Ltd (Avro, makers of the Lancaster) and Vickers-Armstrong, and announced that the CAS wanted 'every endeavour' put forth to prepare a squadron for employing *Upkeep* that spring. An additional 27 Lancasters were to be modified and 150 *Upkeep* weapons produced. The Air Ministry's director of bomber operations, Gp Cpt J. W. Baker, stated that the aircraft and weapons were needed by 1 May so as to allow sufficient training for use against the Ruhr dams by 26 May, when the Ruhr reservoirs would be at their fullest. *Upkeep* would have priority over other Lancaster projects so Avro could make all the internal modifications to the airframes and Vickers would mount all the external *Upkeep*-related hardware and complete technical drawings of the weapon.

With only two months between the go order and the target date, March was a whirlwind of activity for all involved. Wallis started work the day after the decision meeting, and it took him a week to complete the technical drawings for the weapon and send them to Vickers' fabrication facility at Barrow. At this point, Wallis envisaged a wooden-cased spherical projectile with its poles cut flat to fit the carrying cradle's callipers. The actual explosive

The weapon: the *Upkeep* anti-dam depth charge, minus its spherical wooden casing. Referred to as a 'mine' in the RAF's elaborate disinformation campaign, it was colloquially known as the 'bouncing bomb'. (UK National Archives Photo AIR 14/840)

device was a steel cylinder almost 60in. (1.52m) long, tailored to fit the width of the Lancaster's bomb-bay when hung sideways (with the circular ends of the cylinder forming the flattened poles of the sphere). This supersized depth charge was to be encased in 'great staves of wood' secured by six 1.5in. (38mm) steel bands, giving it an overall circumference of 7.5ft (2.29m).

Meanwhile, Avro completed the technical drawings for the modified Type 464 Provisioning Lancaster (the type number referred to the Vickers-Armstrong project number and the misleading terminology referred to the intention that the aircraft could be returned to standard fit after the special operation). The modifications would focus on removing the long, heavy bomb-bay doors and building a fairing over the fore and aft ends, leaving an opening for the weapon.

To hold the 11,960lb (5,425kg) weapon a pair of large, heavy cast-aluminium V-shaped braces would be mounted on the fuselage sides just beneath the wing, hinged at the attach points and spring-loaded to swing outwards when released. A free-rotating 20in. (0.5m) disk was mounted within the arms' angle to clutch the device. The right-hand disk was connected via a 195in. (4.95m) belt to a Vickers-Jassey hydraulic motor (mounted in the forward end of the bomb bay) to provide 500rpm backspin (reverse rotation around the axis perpendicular to the longitudinal axis of the aircraft). These modifications resulted in an increase in empty weight of 1,178lb (534kg) over the original design.

**MARCH 31
1943**

**No 617 Sqn
begins low-level
navigation
training**

In the event, the Air Ministry ordered 23 Lancasters modified to Type 464 standard – three for *Upkeep* trials and 20 to equip a single special squadron, yet to be identified. The first Type 464 Lancaster (ED765/G) arrived at Royal Aircraft Establishment (RAE) Farnborough on 8 April, the second (ED817/G) at RAF Manston (along with 20 concrete-filled inert and four 'live' *Upkeeps*) 12 days later; the third (ED825/G) was sent to the Aeroplane and Armament Experimental Establishment (A&AEE) at Boscombe Down.

The *Upkeep* trials would be undertaken off the very secluded Reculver beach on the north Kent coast. This RAF bombing range was located in a broad bay dominated by an ancient Norman abbey on a promontory, and was backed by steeply sloping dairy pastures with no private houses overlooking the sea.

Trials began on 13 April with the Wellington and one Lancaster (ED765/G) dropping three inert *Upkeeps*. Among the observers on the beach were Acting Wg Cdr Guy Gibson and his bombing leader, Flight Lieutenant (Flt Lt) Robert 'Bob' Hay, DFC, RAAF. In all three cases the wooden casing shattered on impact with the water, although the internal steel cylinders did bound along for a considerable distance.

In the second set of test drops five days later, two spheres sank and the third shattered, with the steel cylinder bouncing along for 700yd (640m) before sinking beneath the waves. Wallis now conceded that the wooden casing was unworkable and that the device would have to be dropped as a bare metal cylinder. This was barely four weeks before the mission.

Gibson was present again at the fourth set of tests (with three tests per set), on 28 April. These tests confirmed that the bare steel cylinder could bounce along the water's surface in an almost perfectly straight line for a distance of 435–670yd (398–613m; all did veer left 30–40ft towards the end of the run), depending on aircraft speed at release. This allowed Wallis to calculate that the 'bouncing bomb' when dropped from 60ft (18.3m) at a speed of 210mph (338km/hr) had an effective range of 476yd (435m). Subsequent tests on 6–12 May, with eight *Upkeeps* dropped, confirmed the required release parameters and that the effective range with no deviations from track was 430–450yd (393–411.5m).

Finally, on 13 May – three days before the launch of *Chastise* – a live *Upkeep* was dropped from a Lancaster at 75ft (22.9m) five miles off Broadstairs. It bounced seven times for more than 700yd (640m), sank and detonated; a second Lancaster filmed all this. The five remaining trials *Upkeeps* were dropped in the sea in the same area two days later.

PLAN AND PRACTICE

'Never has so much been expected of so few.'
Message chalked onto *Upkeep* weapon of 617 Squadron Lancaster AJ–B by Warrant Officer Abram Garshowitz,
RCAF, killed during the Dams Raid, 16–17 May 1943

The men

While Harris followed Portal's directive to proceed with preparing for an attack on the dams, he still refused to withdraw one of his Lancaster squadrons from the ongoing Battle of the Ruhr. Harris elected instead to create a whole new unit, to be formed largely with experienced volunteers.

On 15 March Harris directed the new AOC 5 Group, AVM Cochrane, to establish an as yet undesignated squadron (called 'Squadron X' until a number could be assigned by the Air Staff) and recommended 24-year-old Acting Wg Cdr Guy Gibson as its commander. Cochrane had been 5 Group commander for only two weeks and did not yet know Gibson. Nevertheless, on 18 March Cochrane interviewed Gibson, who had just completed his second Bomber Command tour only a week before. The interview went well and next day Cochrane met with Gibson and Gp Cpt J. N. H. 'Charles' Whitworth, commander of RAF Scampton, to give them the new unit's initial operational tasking – albeit in the sketchiest of terms.

By this time the command's wheels were in motion. What was to become the most famous squadron in the RAF was established on paper on 17 March and designated No 617 Squadron a week later. The unit was to be based at Scampton, a pre-war aerodrome four miles (6.4km) north of Lincoln. A Bomber Command base normally had two squadrons assigned, but in order to permit the construction of concrete runways the station had recently been vacated by 49 Sqn. This allowed, at least temporarily, ample space for aircraft parking, barracks, hangars, offices and shopfloors for the new unit. Gibson arrived on 21 March to examine his new unit's home and plan the physical establishment.

Three or four days later – while Gibson was in Weybridge receiving his first briefing from Wallis on the *Upkeep* weapon and how it worked and was to be

APRIL 5 1943

No 542 Squadron photo reconnaissance shows Möhne Dam full to capacity

19

ACTING WING COMMANDER GUY PENROSE GIBSON, VC, DSO, DFC

Guy Penrose Gibson was born in Simla, India, in August 1918. The son of a British official in the Indian Forestry Service, he grew up under the 'Raj'. The family were used to having numerous servants over whom even young Guy had authority. This experience perhaps accounts for the rather pronounced prejudices he showed as a commander.

The family returned to England when Guy was six. He was educated at St George's Preparatory School, Felixstowe, and the independent St Edward's School in Oxford. Gibson joined the RAF almost immediately after leaving school, and after flight training – having graduated with average marks – he was posted to 83 Sqn, flying Handley-Page Hampdens. Once war broke out Gibson soon became known for his enthusiasm for operations and he flew as often as possible during the critical summer of 1940. He completed 39 combat missions, and near the end of that tour was awarded the DFC and promoted to flight-lieutenant.

Despite his arrogance and outspokenness, Gibson was socially astute and politically adept and soon endeared himself to his commanders with his brazen aggressiveness and implacable attitude towards those who were not so 'gung-ho'. Consequently, when he was posted to Fighter Command's 29 Sqn the AOC 5 Group, AVM Sir Arthur Harris, assured him he would return to Bomber Command 'in the fullness of time'.

Flying a radar-equipped Bristol Beaufighter IF nightfighter, Gibson was officially credited with having 'destroyed three and damaged a fourth enemy aircraft' during 99 combat sorties. True to his word, when Harris took over as AOC-in-C Bomber Command he 'rescued' Gibson from a posting to 51 Operational Training Unit as a nightfighter instructor. Harris promoted Gibson well

ahead of his peers, to acting wing commander – on the same day that the RAF had promoted him to permanent squadron leader. Harris also encouraged the new AOC 5 Group, AVM Sir John Slessor, to find a suitable leadership position for the young prodigy.

Given command of 106 Sqn, Gibson 'led from the front', logging four missions in the ill-starred Manchester and another 25 in Lancasters. During this period Gibson was credited with improving the serviceability of the chronically problematic Manchester so that his unit was the best of the eight RAF units operating this type. He was the first to fully equip his aircraft with cameras to assess bombing accuracy. Slessor showcased Gibson's success during a visit by Sir Archibald Sinclair, the Secretary of State for Air, and other VIPs, thus making Gibson well known at the highest levels of the air force.

Gibson was by his own admission biased against NCO pilots, and he also exhibited disdain towards 'other-ranks' aircrew, as well as ground crew and other non-operational types (to one NCO ground crewman, Gibson was a 'bumptious little bastard'). He relished the company of officer-class professionals among the men he flew with – men from the same social class as himself. For him, his young, aggressive peers 'gladly went to war in bombers, took great pride in their performance and were not deflected from their purpose by the inherent dangers of their trade'. This, in turn, engendered a strong sense of camaraderie and allegiance among those of his inner circle. Collegial respect and mutual admiration created a cadre of exceptional officer-pilots who followed him to do the extraordinary.

delivered – the first 14 Lancaster crews were posted into the new unit. Five – two of them captained by NCO pilots – transferred 'across the aerodrome' from the co-located 57 Sqn. In those days a Bomber Command squadron was organized in two flights ('A' and 'B'), each with ten or so aircraft and crews. As a unit received additional aircrew, the men would be formed into a third ('C') flight which would later be used as the basis of a new squadron.

A 617 Sqn Lancaster III dropping an *Upkeep* weapon during practice at Reculver. (IWM FLM 2365)

Commanding 'C' Flight of 57 Sqn was Sqn Ldr Henry Young, DFC and Bar, the 27-year-old son of a London solicitor and an American socialite from southern California. Young had flown 51 operational missions in Western Europe, North Africa and the Mediterranean, with 102 Sqn on Armstrong-Whitworth Whitleys and with 104 Sqn on Wellingtons. On eight of these missions he commanded a ten-aircraft detachment on Malta. During his first tour Young had been forced to ditch twice, on both occasions saving his crew. The fact that he had spent more than 30 hours in the aeroplanes' tiny life-rafts, as well as his fame as an oarsman in Oxford University's 1938 championship rowing team, inevitably led to his acquiring the nickname 'Dinghy'.

Posted at the same time was Gibson's 'B'-Flight commander, 21-year-old Sqn Ldr Henry Maudslay, DFC. A 1940 graduate of Eton College, he was also an oarsman, having been named Captain of Boats in his final year. An experienced instructor, Maudslay had flown 29 operations in Handley-Page Hampdens (44 Sqn) and 16 on Lancasters (1654 Heavy Conversion Unit and 50 Sqn) before arriving at Scampton. Also from 50 Sqn was the talented but relatively inexperienced (26 operations) 22-year-old Pilot Officer Leslie ('Les') Knight, RAAF, and his crew, all of whom volunteered for what sounded like an interesting assignment.

Three crews came from 97 Sqn.

Flt Lt David Maltby, DFC, a reserved but determined 23-year-old graduate of Marlborough College, had flown five operations with 106 Sqn (Hampdens) and 21 with 97 Sqn (Hampdens, Manchesters and Lancasters) before commanding a section in 1485 Target Towing and Gunnery Flight at Scampton. Returning to 97 Sqn on 17 March, Maltby was given a new and inexperienced crew, all fresh from training.

The 6ft 3in. (1.9m), 24-year-old red-headed Flt Lt Joseph 'Big Joe' McCarthy, DFC, was an American from New York City. Having joined the RCAF in May 1941, he had just finished his first operational tour. He and his crew had flown their 27th successful sortie on Lancasters – a raid on St-Nazaire – on 22–23 March.

Relative newcomer Flt Lt John Leslie ('Les') Munro, RNZAF, flew his first operational sortie on 2–3 January 1943. He was an aggressive pilot, and he and his crew completed another 19 missions in the next 11 weeks. Returning from the St-Nazaire raid, they responded to a 5 Group circular 'calling for volunteers from those crews nearing the end of their first operational tour … to form a new squadron to undertake a special mission'.

Towards the end of the month another seven full crews, plus a number of additional personnel to plug gaps in other crews, were posted to the squadron. These included three pilots Gibson knew and personally requested.

Gibson's favourite was 22-year-old Flt Lt John 'Hoppy' Hopgood, DFC and Bar. Hopgood was a Cranwell graduate, a veteran bomber pilot and an experienced Lancaster instructor. Hopgood had flown ten Hampden missions with 50 Sqn as a bomb-aimer/navigator and another 35 as a Manchester/Lancaster captain and instructor with 106 Sqn. While with 106 Sqn Hopgood had taught Gibson to fly the Lancaster four-engined heavy bomber. Hopgood made a strong impression on the commander with his 'press-on spirit'.

Also from 106 Sqn was 21-year-old Flt Lt David Shannon, DFC, RAAF. He had flown five missions as Gibson's second pilot, developing a tight bond with his captain. After completing another 31 operations, Shannon had just obtained a posting to 83 Sqn to join the neophyte Pathfinder Force when Gibson recruited him for 617 Sqn. Only Shannon's navigator, Flying Officer (Fg Off) Danny Walker, DFC, RCAF, followed his captain to Scampton.

Finally, there was Flt Lt Harold 'Mick' Martin, DFC, a 23-year-old Australian in the RAF. He was a veteran of 36 combat operations in two bomber tours, with 455 Sqn RAAF (Hampdens) and 50 Sqn RAF (Manchesters/Lancasters). Gibson had met Martin at a Buckingham Palace medals ceremony where they had discussed the tactical advantages of ultra-low flying. From 1654 Heavy Conversion Unit Martin and his well-experienced crew headed to Scampton, with his bomb-aimer, Flt Lt Bob Hay, becoming 617 Sqn's bombing leader.

In addition to these, Flight-Sergeant (F/Sgt) Kenneth Brown, RCAF, captained one of three additional all-NCO crews also transferred to bring the new unit to its full complement of flying personnel. Just after the briefing for Brown's seventh mission with 44 Sqn – to Berlin on 27–28 March – his commander, Wg Cdr John Nettleton, VC, notified him that upon return he

THE DANN BOMBSIGHT

One of the most critical parameters for delivering Upkeep was to release it at precisely the right distance from the target. It needed to "bounce" three times, each contact with the water's surface allowing the backspin of the weapon to retard its forward velocity. If released too late (inside 425yd/388.6m) when it hit the dam wall the impact forces could destroy the device or cause it to "bounce off" the vertical surface instead of "rolling down" the surface – one key to effective destructive force was physical adherence to the dam wall. If released too early (outside 475yd/434.3m) the device tended to begin veering to the left which then made accurately hitting the centre of the dam – another requirement for effective use of its destructive force – problematic.

Therefore accurate determination of range from the dam wall was a critical parameter – one that was met with a rather simple solution.

This was provided by Wg Cdr Charles L. Dann, the Supervisor of Aeronautics at A&AEE Boscombe Down. Since distance between the Möhne's sluice towers was known, as was optimum release distance, it became a rather simple trigonometry problem. The solution was a small wooden hand-held Y-shaped angular sight.

The 'Dann bombsight' was held by a thick dowel mounted beneath its junction, a peephole was mounted in the base of the stem and a small white dowel projected from the end of each arm, angled apart 29.5 degrees. As the Lancaster approached the target the sluice towers would begin to spread and when they touched the dowels, the weapon was released.

and his crew were 'transferred to a new squadron … and I can do nothing about it'. Saying farewell the next day, Nettleton added encouragingly: 'Brown, you're going to be the backbone of this new squadron.' Brown's wireless operator, Sgt Harry Hewstone, commented upon arriving at Scampton and seeing who were already there: 'Skip, if we're the backbone of this squadron, we must be damn close to the ass end!'

The training

Just as the first crews arrived at Scampton, so did ten Lancaster B Mark Is and IIIs, one each from ten of 5 Group's 15 squadrons operating the type. By the morning of 27 March the full complement of ground crew – 382 men, all from within 5 Group – had arrived, and following aircraft inspections that afternoon the unit was pronounced ready to fly. First off was Flt Lt Bill Astell, who flew his former 50 Sqn Lancaster AJ–B (W4940) at low level for two hours around Leicester, Rugby and Birmingham and 'photographed nine reservoirs' to 'work out cross-country routes for the OTUs'.

That same day a memorandum arrived from 5 Group's SASO, Gp Cpt Harold V. Satterly. It established the training objectives for the new squadron, which were to be met by 10 May. These included accurate navigation under moonlight conditions at 'a height which will best afford security against fighter attack'; 'final approach to the target at 100 feet at [approximately] 240 mph … it will be convenient to practise this over water'; and bomb release to be carried out visually at an estimated range gauged either by landmark on a nearby shore, or by timing a run from a given landmark, to provide an accuracy of about 40yd.

Sqn Ldr Young, Gibson's second-in-command, was responsible for designing the training programme to meet these objectives. Training began on 31 March, with navigation exercises using ten standard three-hour-plus cross-country routes. Initially, for familiarisation purposes, these routes were flown singly in daylight at 700ft (213m). Then they were flown at 200ft (61m) for three days, before 'stepping down' to 150ft (46m). The routes included dead-reckoning legs – involving calculation of heading, airspeed and time – over the North Sea, and flights across the countryside to various English, Scottish or Welsh lakes that required map-reading. As individual proficiency increased the routes were flown in pairs, and finally in three-aircraft formations at night.

To simulate moonlight conditions a system known as 'two-stage blue' was adopted from the US Army Air Forces. This involved placing blue celluloid panels over the windscreen, cockpit side-windows and gunners' glazed areas, and aircrew wearing amber-lensed flying goggles. Five squadron bombers used this training modification, the first arriving on 11 April.

Not all the crews met the exacting standards required by the mission and the squadron commander. By mid-April Gibson had sent Young's two NCO crews back to 57 Sqn because they or one of their members 'did not come up to the standard necessary for this squadron'. These crews were replaced by a single crew only: that of Plt Off William Divall, who had joined 57 Sqn less than two months before. All this reduced 617 Sqn's strength from 22 crews to 21.

Even harder to achieve than successful low-level navigation by moonlight was the risky requirement to hold an exact altitude close to the water in the dark. Gibson became personally acquainted with this on 28 March when he, Hopgood and Young flew mock attacks on Derwent Reservoir after dusk and almost came to grief. After Gibson recounted this harrowing experience to Satterly, the Group SASO contacted MAP's director of scientific research (DSR) to ask about a solution. The new DSR, the later Sir Benjamin Lockspeiser, recalled a 1941 Coastal Command experiment with Lockheed Hudson patrol bombers aimed at helping with depth-charging U-boats at night in shallow, inshore waters. This method used triangulating spotlights mounted on the aircraft. Lockspeiser found the experiment had been deemed a failure because inshore waters were too choppy, but he became convinced that the technique would be more effective over smooth-surfaced lakes. A series of tests was undertaken by RAE Farnborough, and Lockspeiser soon came up with what was officially called the 'spotlight altimeter calibrator'.

The device comprised two Aldis lamps, one mounted in the forward camera aperture under the nose and the other in the disused ventral gun position aft of the bomb bay. The forward lamp or spotlight (shrouded in a length of 'stovepipe' to shield the light from enemy gunners) was pointed downwards, perpendicular to the longitudinal axis of the aircraft and starboard 30°, and shone a 10°-wide beam of light downwards forward of the starboard propellers. The aft spotlight was angled forward about 20° from the perpendicular and outwards 40° so that the two beams crossed (but did not intersect) at the prescribed altitude under the bomber's belly. The aircraft would be at the correct altitude at the point when, viewed from the starboard cockpit blister, the two pools of light touched to form a 'figure eight' on the surface below.

It would be the navigator's job to watch the pools of light get closer as the aircraft descended over the lake and call 'steady' when they touched. To help the pilot maintain that height a second altimeter was mounted atop the Lancaster's glare shield, within the pilot's field of vision when looking at the target through the windscreen. After the pilot set the barometric pressure to get the indicator needle to point to 60ft (18.3m), he would simply hold the needle steady in order to maintain the prescribed height.

On 4 April Maudslay flew one of the squadron's loaned Lancasters, AJ–Z (W4926), to RAE Farnborough, where the spotlights were mounted. Four days later, after testing the system over the sea, Maudslay returned to Scampton and demonstrated the system by flying along the runway at low

Lancaster 'P-for-Popsie' (ED909) taxying out on a *Chastise* practice sortie. This aircraft was the first Type 464 Provisioning Lancaster to arrive at 617 Sqn and was flown by Flt Lt 'Mick' Martin and his crew. (IWM MH 6540)

**APRIL 8
1943**

**First Type 464
Lancaster
(ED765/G)
arrives at RAE
Farnborough**

level in the dark. The squadron's electricians quickly mounted the lamps on three other bombers. After flying down the runway to have their lights calibrated and heights confirmed by theodolite, over the next few nights the crews began training with this simple, reliable way to safely maintain low altitude over water.

By 26 April Wallis had worked out the final *Upkeep* delivery parameters – from 450yd (± 25yd, or 411.5m ± 22.9m) range and 60ft (18.3m) height at 220mph (354km/h) – and informed Gibson accordingly. Over the following week the squadron concentrated on weapons delivery practice, dropping 10lb or 20lb (4.5/9.1kg) tetrachloride 'smoke bombs' on Wainfleet Range, on the Wash on England's east coast. A total of 168 practice attacks were made using the newly developed Dann bombsight and aiming between two 30ft x 20ft (9.1m x 6.1m) white 'cricket boards' standing some 700ft (213m) apart; 284 bombs were dropped with an average error of 39ft (11.9m).

Having met 5 Group's training standards, from 4 May the squadron graduated to 'large force employment' (LFE) exercises: operating ten-aircraft 'packages' nightly and simulating attacks from 60ft (18.3m) mainly against the dam at Eyebrook Reservoir, two miles (3.2km) south of Uppingham in the English east midlands. To facilitate these simulations, two pairs of 20ft x 12ft (6.1m x 3.7m) canvas targets, connected by a camouflage 'scrim', were mounted on the dam's parapet, positioned apart so as to represent the two sluice towers of the Möhne Dam.

The aircraft

The first two Type 464 Provisioning Lancasters arrived at Scampton on 21 April. The most noticeable modification, to the bomb bay, made the great Avro heavy bomber look 'disembowelled', and prompted some squadron members to refer to them irreverently as 'abortions'.

Another obvious modification was the deletion of the mid-upper turret. The aircraft would be ingressing beneath the Luftwaffe's radar coverage, so interception by night fighters would be avoided. This allowed the upper turret to be sacrificed so as to compensate somewhat for the increased drag caused by the gaping bomb bay.

A Lancaster crew normally consisted of seven men (an eighth man, a 'second pilot', might be temporarily included as a way of increasing his experience before he became a bomber captain). The bomb-aimer would man the forward turret until the initial point on the bomb run was approached, at which time he

The delivery vehicle: Avro Lancaster B Mk III ED825/G, showing modifications to facilitate carrying the *Upkeep* anti-dam weapon. The B.III was virtually identical to the original B.I but was powered by the 1649-cubic-inch (27-litre) V-12 supercharged Merlin 28, licence-built by the USA's Packard Motor Car Company. This engine produced the same 1,390hp as the Rolls Royce original. (IWM Photo ATP 11384B)

Avro Lancaster B.III Type 474 Provisioning

Serial number	Sent to	Date	617 Sqn code	Fate and remarks
ED765	RAE Farnborough	8 April	–	Lost in training accident, 5 August 1943
	RAF Scampton	July	AJ–M	
ED817	RAF Manston	20 April	–	Not flown on Dams Raid. SOC** Lossiemouth, early 1947
	RAF Scampton	16 May	AJ–C*	
ED825	A&AEE Boscombe Down	22 April	–	Flown on Dams Raid as AJ–T Shot down 10–11 December 1943
	RAF Scampton	16 May	AJ–T	
ED864	RAF Scampton	22 April	AJ–B	Lost on Dams Raid
ED865	RAF Scampton	22 April	AJ–S	Shot down on Dams Raid
ED886	RAF Scampton	21 April	AJ–O	Shot down 10–11 December 1943
ED887	RAF Scampton	22 April	AJ–A	Shot down on Dams Raid
ED906	RAF Scampton	23 April	AJ–J	SOC** Scampton, July 1947
ED909	RAF Scampton	21 April	AJ–P	As above
ED910	RAF Scampton	25 April	AJ–C	Shot down on Dams Raid
ED912	RAF Scampton	1 May	AJ–N	SOC** Lossiemouth, Sept 1946
ED915	RAF Scampton	25 April	AJ–Q	Ground abort on Dams Raid. SOC** Lossiemouth, 8 October 1946
ED918	RAF Scampton	28 April	AJ–F	Lost in training, 20 January 1944
ED921	RAF Scampton	27 April	AJ–W	SOC** Lossiemouth, early 1947
ED924	RAF Scampton	29 April	AJ–Y	As above
ED925	RAF Scampton	28 April	AJ–M	Shot down on Dams Raid
ED927	RAF Scampton	1 May	AJ–E	Lost on Dams Raid
ED929	RAF Scampton	30 April	AJ–L	SOC** Lossiemouth, early 1947
ED932	RAF Scampton	30 April	AJ–G	SOC** Scampton, July 1947
ED933	RAF Scampton	2 May	AJ–H	Damaged 12 May; not on raid
ED934	RAF Scampton	1 May	AJ–K	Shot down on Dams Raid
ED936	RAF Scampton	2 May	AJ–X	Lost on landing, 28 July 1944
ED937	RAF Scampton	4 May	AJ–Z	Shot down on Dams Raid

* ED817 arrived at Scampton during the late afternoon of 16 May, too late to be loaded with Upkeep as a spare for the Dams Raid. The aircraft was coded AJ-C after the raid (the original AJ-C having failed to return).

** SOC: struck off charge and scrapped at locality stated.

would descend to crouch over the bombsight and determine the release of ordnance. However, delivery of *Upkeep* involved a low-level frontal attack, which meant the front-turret guns were needed to suppress enemy anti-aircraft fire at the same time as the bomb-aimer was busy peering at the target through his Dann bombsight. Consequently, for this mission the mid-upper turret gunner was moved to the front turret. A further small modification – installing a set of stirrups beneath the turret – was needed to prevent the gunner's feet bumping the bomb-aimer while he was concentrating on navigation or bomb-aiming.

In fact, the bomb-aimer's workload was greatly increased due to the fact that ingress and egress as well as the actual attack would be at ultra-low level. At such heights the navigator's view of the ground immediately below and to each side was considerably restricted. Consequently the bomb-aimer, who had a more panoramic view from the nose, was tasked with helping the pilot keep the aircraft on the desired ground track. To facilitate this each bomb-aimer prepared a route map of his own. Some made 'strip maps'

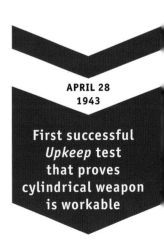

APRIL 28 1943

First successful *Upkeep* test that proves cylindrical weapon is workable

mounted on rollers to dispense with having to constantly unfold and refold large charts in the cramped nose compartment. To increase visibility from the nose the new Lancasters featured an enlarged, near-hemispherical Perspex nose bubble in place of the conventional saucer-shaped dome (which was in fact little more than a porthole).

The final aircraft modification was in the radiotelephone (R/T) system. The Dams Raid would be the first to employ the 'master-bomber' concept, whereby a single airborne commander would direct the individual attacks and reorganise the strike force as needed to ensure the primary targets were destroyed first. However, it soon became clear during the low-altitude formation and LFE practices at Eyebrook that the Lancaster's standard TR1154/55 wireless sets would not suffice. Again, RAE was asked to help. Its radio department decided to replace the existing sets with the more reliable TR1143 very-high-frequency (VHF) radios normally used in RAF fighters. Flt Lt Bernard Bone was sent to Scampton with a 35-man team from 26 (Signals) Group to install them, completing the work by 9 May.

The weapon

On 25 March, in a cunning attempt to mask the true nature of *Upkeep* and its intended targets, the Air Ministry's director of intelligence (security) began a disinformation campaign so effective that it has subsequently deceived even most historians. The 'cover story' maintained that 'the weapon is a special type of mine and the [spherical] wooden casing is designed for use in localities where it will be handled by native labour [implying employment outside of Europe]. The spinning device is in connection with the fusing which is effected by centrifugal force. The uses of the weapon are in the main anti-submarine ... Units armed with the weapon are to be known as Special Mining Squadrons.'

When the first of 96 *Upkeep* weapons – 40 concrete-filled 'training rounds' and 56 'live rounds' – began arriving at Scampton at the start of May, they were referred to as 'mines'. This usage has continued ever since. In the meantime, of course, Wallis had forsaken the spherical wooden casing. The weapon was in fact a 9,250lb (4,196kg) cylindrical depth charge.

Because the *Upkeep* weapon was no longer spherical, it would have to be released in a wings-level (zero-bank) attitude. If released within Wallis' precisely prescribed parameters of height, range, speed, rotation and aircraft attitude, *Upkeep* would skip three times, the backspin providing sufficient retardation so that the weapon would contact the target with an impact 'soft' enough to prevent disabling damage to the weapon but with enough residual rotational moment to cause it to 'roll down' the dam wall at 10–20fps (3–6m/sec). At a depth of 30ft (9.1m), three standard Royal Navy Mk XIV hydrostatic pistols – water-pressure sensor triggers – would detonate the 6,600lb (2,994kg) of Torpex underwater (torpedo) explosive.

In case the weapon did not sink to the required depth – or somehow became deposited on dry land – a 90-second timer provided a 'self-destruct' fuse.

Squadron training with *Upkeep* began on 11 May, when Gibson led Hopgood and Martin to Manston to load training rounds and then flew to

Reculver to practise deliveries, aiming at two screens erected onshore – near the abbey – to simulate the Möhne's sluice towers. The following day Shannon's, Knight's and Munro's crews flew the same exercises, with Maudslay's and other crews doing so next day. All participants were well aware that release at extremely low altitude was imperative: the angle of contact with the water had to be shallow enough (less than 7° angle of incidence) to cause the device to 'skip' along the surface. Some pilots were a bit over-zealous: two Lancasters were damaged by a huge spray of water and shingle engulfing the tail. Maudslay's aircraft, AJ–X (ED933), was damaged to such an extent that it had to be withdrawn for repair. He was assigned AJ–Z as a replacement, reducing the *Chastise* strike force to 19 bombers.

On 14 May Gibson and Young organised a final, four-hour, near full-scale 'dress rehearsal'. By this time Gibson had decided which crews would attack which dams and the practice was organised accordingly. Nine crews in three triple-aircraft formations navigated first to Eyebrook ('Target A') to simulate attacking the Möhne, then to Abberton Reservoir just south of Colchester ('Target B') to simulate attacking the Eder. Gibson coordinated individual attacks using the new VHF radios. Six other crews followed another route and simulated attacks against the Derwent Dam, near Sheffield ('Target C'). Finally the remaining crews – the 'mobile reserve' – practised at Wainfleet Range.

The targets

Targets were selected by a new *ad hoc* committee that met for the first time on 18 March. The meeting was convened by ACM Portal and chaired by his ACAS (Operations), AVM Bottomley, who three years before had authored Portal's request to the Air Ministry to develop the means to breach the Möhne. Bottomley had ostensibly been commissioned to oversee the development and employment of *Upkeep* and its unsuccessful 'little brother', *Highball*, which was to have been used by Coastal Command Mosquitoes against Axis capital ships. Bottomley took a generous view of *Chastise*'s charter because of his own – and his chief's – personal interest in the project.

The committee determined that 'the two most important dams vulnerable to attack in Germany are the Möhne and the Eder'. Breaching the Eder would not affect the Ruhr industrial district, but being similar to the Möhne in construction, it was potentially vulnerable to *Upkeep*. The committee ruled out the Sorpe – an earthen berm-type dam that held back the second-largest reservoir affecting the Ruhr – as 'unsuitable for attack, for tactical and technical reasons'.

When an independent Ministry of Economic Warfare (MEW) study recommending destruction of the Möhne and Sorpe – and not the Eder – came to Bottomley's attention, he consulted with Col C. G. Vickers, VC, and MEW analyst O. L. Lawrence. Lawrence opined that destroying both the Möhne and the Sorpe 'would be worth much more than twice the destruction of one'. However, the Eder Dam, the water from which flowed through Kassel into the Weser-und-Mittelland-Kanal, was of 'no major economic

The first primary target: the Möhne Dam, as seen in an RAF vertical overhead aerial reconnaissance photo. At this stage in weapon development and mission planning, pictures like these were about as much hard intelligence about the target that the RAF possessed. Note the double row of anti-torpedo nets separated by timber 'spreaders' positioned well in front of the dam structure. North is at top of the photo. (IWM Photo C 3717)

importance'. Bottomley was convinced and, assured that *Upkeep* 'had very good prospects' of breaching the Sorpe also, he recommended to Portal that simultaneous attacks should be made against the Möhne and Sorpe, with the Eder to be attacked if circumstances allowed.

Consequently, on 29 March, when Gibson travelled to 5 Group HQ – St Vincents, an imposing 78-year-old building set among trees at the edge of Grantham in Lincolnshire – AVM Cochrane informed Gibson that the primary targets of 617 Sqn's first operation were the Möhne and Sorpe dams. Next day Gibson journeyed again to Weybridge where Wallis informed him how *Upkeep* was expected to work against the Möhne. However, Wallis was somewhat reserved regarding the prospects for breaching the Sorpe.

The Möhne-Talsperre, located some 30 miles (48km) east of the location of the main Ruhr industries, was the largest dam in Europe. Completed in 1913, it was 2,549ft (777m) across and 120ft (36.6m) tall, from bedrock to crest. It held back 140 million tons of water reportedly needed for 'drinking purposes and industrial supplies'. There were also 13 hydro-electric power stations downstream. These target considerations paled, however, next to the potential amount of destruction resulting from the deluge inundating the valley – sweeping away structures, flooding factories and washing away barges. It was calculated that the Möhnesee would empty in ten hours, which would 'cause a disaster of the first magnitude even in the lower reaches of the Ruhr'.

Just six miles (9.7km) south-southwest of the Möhne was the Sorpe-Talsperre, comprising an earthen berm 2,100ft (640m) long that rose 200ft (61m) above the streambed. On both sides a gently sloping embankment stabilised a watertight central concrete core. At 30ft depth on the lakeward side the bank the berm, consisting of granulated rock and hard-packed earth, was 67.5ft (20.6m) thick; this would absorb much of *Upkeep*'s explosive force. Nevertheless, Wallis initially calculated that the pressure wave resulting from a detonation would displace the central core by 16–20 inches (40–51cm) – enough to crack the watertight seal. It was hoped that a serious leak would cause sufficient erosion of the gravel and earth on the far side of the dam to cause the eventual collapse of the central core due to lack of support on that side.

ACM Harris, never an optimist about this operation, thought the Sorpe attack had 'a poor chance for success'. In fact, even Wallis lost confidence in the approach here. He requested a preliminary, conventional bombing attack against the Sorpe's far side so as to weaken it sufficiently for *Upkeep* to work. However, this was viewed, rightly, as alerting the enemy to the real attack and Wallis' request was denied. Disappointed, Wallis commented during his portion of the mission briefing that 'it would need at least six mines to crack' the Sorpe.

Despite these drawbacks, the Sorpe was still considered a worthy target because it held back another 70 million tons of water. If the dam was breached

MAY 4–7 1943

No 617 Sqn conducts ten-aircraft 'large force employment' exercises

the deluge would contribute greatly to the desired impact on the Ruhr basin. Therefore, the diversionary force would attack the Sorpe using a weapon actually designed for a different type of target, and hope for the best.

Meanwhile, because there probably would be *Upkeep* weapons remaining after breaching the Möhne, Gibson wanted the Eder included as a primary target. Rather than use these weapons against the Sorpe, he wanted to take on the Eder since the attack profile was the same as for the Möhne and the chances of success were much greater.

The Eder-Talsperre was indeed very similar to the Möhne. Built at the same time, it was located 46 miles

(74km) east-southeast of the Möhne and produced the largest reservoir in Germany. Spanning a deep, narrow valley, it was 145ft (44m) high and 1,290ft (393m) across. The attack profile was greatly complicated by the surrounding high terrain. The dam held back 200 million tons of water, and breaching it would provide a dramatic – if militarily inconsequential – flood downstream, through Kassel.

The second primary target: Eder Dam, as seen in an RAF vertical aerial reconnaissance photo used for mission planning, preparation and briefing. While RAF planners considered the Sorpe the next most important target to strike, 5 Group OpOrd specified the Eder as the second target, assigning the Sorpe to the diversionary force. (IWM Photo C 3718)

The plan

Planning Operation *Chastise* was the personal responsibility of 5 Group's SASO, Gp Capt Satterly, who initially outlined the concept of operations – along with the squadron's training objectives – in 'most secret' orders to Gibson on 27 March.

As *Upkeep* was perfected, aircrews trained and the concept of how the weapon was to be employed was refined, the draft operations plan was outlined in a briefing to AVM Bottomley's committee on 5 May – a meeting also attended by Wallis. Wallis stressed the point that, for maximum effect, the water level of the Möhnesee needed to be within 5ft (1.7m) of the dam's crest. Disturbed that water was already being drawn off, Wallis urged that *Chastise* be implemented at the earliest opportunity. Cochrane agreed, wanting to strike as soon as possible after 14–15 May – in clear weather and under the full moon.

Five days later, Satterly completed a handwritten draft operation order (OpOrd) and sent it to Whitworth and Gibson for comment. Two days later, capitalising on the lessons of six weeks of intense training, practice and trials, Gibson responded with numerous recommendations. Satterly incorporated many of them, though not all.

The plan called for 20 bombers to make a succession of individual attacks on the five Ruhr dams, plus the Eder and Diemel. To do this, 617 Sqn would be split into three waves: a main force of nine bombers to attack the primary targets, namely the Möhne (Target 'X') and Eder (Target 'Y'); a diversionary force of five aircraft to attack the secondary targt, the Sorpe (Target 'Z'); and a reserve force of six aircraft to attack the first pair again or strike the tertiary targets ('D'–'G', formally called 'targets of last resort'), depending on the results achieved by the earlier waves.

MAY 1 1943

First *Upkeep* weapons arrive at RAF Scampton

Since the German nightfighters (*Nachtjägder*) were most successful at full moon, Bomber Command had no significant concurrent operations planned. The only operations were the following: eight Mosquitoes were to make nuisance raids against four major German cities while others conducted intruder operations over six Luftwaffe bases in the Netherlands; and 54 Lancasters, Stirlings and Wellingtons would drop mines in the German Bight while another ten dropped leaflets in France.

All this meant 617 Sqn would have to provide its own diversionary effort. It was planned for the main and diversionary forces to cross the enemy coast simultaneously at widely separated points – the main force over the Scheldt Estuary, the diversionary force over the Dutch Frisian Islands.

The plan was that the two forces would arrive at their targets at midnight (midnight being the assigned time over target or 'TOT'). The diversionary force would have to depart Scampton first due to the longer distance to the coast and to the force's target. The main force would be under Gibson's direct control; he would coordinate individual attacks via VHF. Taking off 2½ hours later than the main force, the reserve force would be under HQ 5 Group control; each bomber would be directed, via Morse code sent via long-range wireless/telegraphy (W/T), to attack specifically assigned targets.

At 0900 on Saturday, 15 May, AVM Bottomley sent the 'warning order' to 5 Group directing: 'Operation *Chastise*. Immediate attack of targets "X", "Y", "Z" approved. Execute at first suitable opportunity.' Cochrane informed Whitworth that the attack would be launched the next evening.

The Type 464 Lancasters were stood down (except for air-test sorties) to allow last-minute maintenance. Wallis arrived at Scampton to monitor the loading and arming of weapons. The laborious process of loading involved a ten-ton crane, six modified bomb trolleys and two mobile gantries, which limited the loading rate to about one *Upkeep* an hour. Meanwhile, Gibson travelled to Grantham to confer with Cochrane on the final details of the mission and publish the OpOrd for the squadron. At this point the Hennesee-Talsperre was deleted from the target list due to its proximity to Meschede, a small industrial town thought to be well defended; instead, Diemel was made Target 'F'.

At 1800 these three key individuals – Wallis, Gibson and Cochrane – plus Young, Maudslay, Hopgood (Gibson's deputy mission commander for ingress and for the Möhne attacks), and Hay, gathered at Whitworth's quarters for the initial mission briefing. Hopgood suggested the routing around the Ruhr be adjusted to the north so as to avoid Hüls, where a rubber factory was also thought to be well defended.

The target realignment was incorporated into Satterly's product, which became 'No. 5 Group Operation Order No. B.976' – with appendices for 'Routes and Timings', 'Signals Procedure for Target Diversions' and 'Light and Moon Tables' – and was promulgated at 1000 the next morning.

The scale model of the Möhne Dam and its surrounding area, photographed from an oblique angle as if from the north. The model, used in the briefing for the mission, may still be seen at the Imperial War Museum, London. (IWM Photo MH 842)

'The longest briefing I ever attended'

Shortly after noon on Sunday, 16 May, crew members began to be briefed on their specific duties for the mission. Gibson and Wallis met with the pilots and navigators while 5 Group chief signals officer Wg Cdr Wally Dunn met with the wireless operators.

Two of the 21 crews were not included: Plt Off Bill Divall had a knee injury and Flt Lt Harry Wilson was ill. Thus, there were 19 crews for 19 aircraft. The third prototype aircraft, ED825, was flown in from Boscombe Down as a spare, loaded with an *Upkeep* and coded AJ–T, but there was not time to mount the TR1143 radio or the spotlight altimeter. The second prototype, ED817, was also flown to Scampton but arrived too late to be loaded.

At this point the targets were finally revealed – to the relief of those who feared they would be up against the mighty *Tirpitz* – and after refreshments at 1400 the bomb-aimers and gunners joined the pilots and navigators in viewing large tabletop models of the Möhne and Sorpe dams. Including the Eder as a primary target had been an afterthought, so unfortunately RAF Intelligence was unable to build a tabletop model of this dam in time for the mission briefing. This meant three crews would be attacking a dam with little advanced appreciation of the difficulties involved.

During the discussion the ingress routing change was finally agreed upon and implemented. This verbal modification to the OpOrd resulted in some confusion and exposure to yet another (unknown) concentration of flak during the operation; it also later created uncertainty among many historians.

At 1800 all aircrew gathered in the large meeting room at Scampton's Junior Ranks' Mess for the final briefing. Gibson began by announcing that the squadron was 'to attack the great dams of Germany', then introduced Wallis, who explained how *Upkeep* worked. After that, Cochrane added information on security concerns and provided some motivational remarks.

Next, Gibson briefed the men on the operational details. The main strike force would comprise Gibson's favourites: on his wing would be Hopgood and Martin, with Young and Maudslay leading the next two sections. The three triple-aircraft formations would take off ten minutes apart and head southeast, cross the North Sea on a line intersecting Southwold and the Scheldt Estuary, then turn east to fly between Schouwen and the Walcheren Islands, which were well defended by *Marine-Flakabteilung* 810 with four heavy and three light flak batteries. Similarly, the formations would fly between the Luftwaffe *Nachtjagd* bases of Gilze-Rijen and Eindhoven in the Netherlands. Circumventing the heavily defended Ruhr to the north, Gibson would lead the attackers to the Möhne-Talsperre, the first primary target.

A historically supported military maxim is 'you fight like you train', and because the squadron's LFE exercises had used 'A–B–C' to reference the three main targets, Gibson deviated from the 'X–Y–Z' designations directed by Satterly's OpOrd.

Oblique view of the briefing scale model of the Eder Dam and its surrounding area. The initial point for the attack was the hilltop Waldeck Castle at the end of the road complex along the right edge of the photograph and the model. As the picture makes clear, the attack profile was very tight indeed. Unfortunately this model was not actually completed in time for the briefing. (IWM Photo MH 27710)

MAY 11–13
1943

No 617 Sqn
conducts *Upkeep*
weapon delivery
practice at
Reculver, Kent

Operation *Chastise* codewords, numbers and letters and their meanings

Codeword	Meaning					
Cooler	617 Sqn aircraft callsign for Operation *Chastise*					
Pranger	Attack Möhne Dam					
Nigger	Möhne breached; divert to Eder					
Dinghy	Eder breached; divert to Sorpe					
Tulip	Cooler 2 take over at Möhne					
	Cooler 4 take over at Eder					
Gilbert	Attack last-resort targets as detailed					
Mason	All aircraft return to base (RTB)					
Goner	*Upkeep* released and …		with (results noted)		in (target)	
	1	failed to explode	8	no apparent breach	A	Möhne
	2	overshot dam	9	small breach	B	Eder
	3	exploded 100+ yd from dam	10	large breach	C	Sorpe
	4	exploded 100yd from dam			D	Lister
	5	exploded 50yd from dam			E	Ennepe
	6	exploded 5yd from dam			F	Diemel
	7	exploded in contact with dam				

Example: 'Goner 710A' indicates '*Upkeep* released and exploded in contact with dam with large breach in Möhne.'

Once Target 'A' was breached, Gibson would lead his remaining bombers to Target 'B', the Eder. If any weapons were left over after these attacks, the remaining armed Lancasters would attack the Sorpe Dam (Target 'C').

The diversionary force would be flown by 'crews who did not reach the highest standards of accuracy in practice'. Gibson and Cochrane felt that 'the attack method against this dam [the Sorpe] was simpler' and thus could be flown by the less proficient crews.

The remaining five crews – including all of Gibson's least favoured, the NCO pilots – would not depart Scampton until after midnight, thus allowing time for reports from the first two groups to provide specific information on which target to attack. This group would fly the same route as the main strike force and, without any directions otherwise, attempt further attacks on targets 'A' and 'B'. However, they also had to be ready to navigate to and deliver their *Upkeep* weapons against any of the three tertiary targets, if necessary. These targets were the Lister ('D'), the Ennepe ('E') and the Diemel ('F').

To enable 'real-time' target assignment changes – directing individual aircraft to attack different targets based on the initial results – specific codewords would be used to indicate when the *Upkeep* was released ('Goner') and to indicate a results assessment (two to three digits) at a specific target (letters 'A' to 'F'). Based on this information, HQ 5 Group would assign targets to the reserve crews using callsigns and codewords to designate a specific target to each aircraft.

While the level of flexibility planned is admirable, saddling the youngest, least-proficient crews with the need to memorise attack data for five possible alternative targets – and remember it for hours afterwards – did have a deleterious effect on mission performance. In the event, most of the reserve force was directed to attack the only target not discussed in its portion of the OpOrd: the Sorpe.

THE RAID

'Not a beautifully planned operation: all of it was very much fit and make fit, despite what has been said afterwards.'

Anonymous member of 617 Sqn who flew on the Dams Raid, 16–17 May 1943.

Diversionary force departs first: 2128–2201

The diversionary force was to be led by the American, Flt Lt Joe McCarthy. This formation's ingress routing was initially eastbound across the North Sea, then turning southwards at the Dutch Frisian Islands, across the IJsselmeer and into the Ruhr region from the north, hopefully distracting the Luftwaffe's *Himmelbett* ('Four-Poster Bed') radar and air defence network in that 'off-axis' direction.

However, in the event, one member of the diversionary force – the leader – was unavoidably delayed. Climbing into the cockpit of AJ–Q ('Q-for-Queenie', nicknamed 'Queenie Chuck Chuck'), Flt Lt McCarthy and his flight engineer, Sgt William Radcliffe, RCAF, completed their extensive pre-flight checks and started the four Merlins. Once they had warmed up (with oil temperature above 40°C) and completed the remaining pre-flight checks, Radcliffe pushed up the throttles for the final run-up check. At this point the number-four (starboard-outer) engine developed a glycol (coolant) leak. As others shut down to await the 2100 'engine start for takeoff', McCarthy informed his crew of their problem, and they gathered their mission gear and scrambled over to the spare aircraft: the newly arrived 'T-for-Tommy'.

Consequently, at 2128 it was Flt Lt R. N. G. 'Norm' Barlow, RAAF, who led off (in AJ–E), followed at one-minute intervals by Flt Lt Les Munro (AJ–W), Plt Off V. W. 'Vern' Byers (AJ–K) and Plt Off Geoff Rice (AJ–H). By the time McCarthy had pre-flighted AJ–T – in the process discovering the absence of a compass deviation card, which caused further delay – then cranked engines and taxied out for takeoff, even the main strike force had broken ground and was headed southeast for the primary targets. 'T-for-Tommy' lifted off at 2201, some 33 minutes late, flying at full throttle in order to make up lost time.

MAY 13 1943

Only live test of *Upkeep*

Two minutes before sunset Flt Lt Norm Barlow lifted AJ–E from Scampton's grass runway and turned it eastbound, at the start of a mission that would become legendary. (IWM Photo CH 18006)

The first four Lancasters flew in a long, in-trail formation – at around 50ft (15.25m) and at a cruising speed of 180mph (290km/h), with about three miles (4.8km) between aircraft. Sunset was at 2130 Double British Summer Time (DBST; GMT +2 hours) on 16 May 1943, but due to the high latitude darkness would not be complete until 2300, so for some time the pilots could still see the aircraft ahead. Eventually, the eastward progression and enveloping dusk finally caused the aircraft to disappear into a gathering gloom.

The Dutch Frisian Islands chain was defended by seven batteries of AA guns from *Marine-Flakabteilung* 246 (MF 246) of the German Navy (Kriegsmarine). RAF intelligence believed the westernmost islands, Texel and Vlieland, were lightly defended. The routing for the diversionary force took the aircraft to a point just north of Vlieland so that they could keep their distance from *Marine-Flakabteilung* 808 (with one 105mm, two 88mm and one 40mm batteries) defending Den Helder, the location of a large naval base occupied until 1940 by the Royal Dutch Navy. Here, the diversionary force would turn southeastwards, overflying Vlieland and then the IJsselmeer. While Texel was in fact at this time undefended, MF 246's third battery was stationed on the west side of Vlieland with two 20mm and four 105mm SKC/32 AA guns.

At 2255, 'E-for-Easy' made the turn on schedule and roared across Vlieland, its sudden appearance surprising the Kriegsmarine flak gunners and alerting them to the approach of the following Lancasters. One minute later 'W-for-Willie' (ED921) had almost cleared the island when it received a flurry of 20mm hits that tore a hole in the aircraft's side and knocked out the VHF wireless transmitter, intercom, master compass and rear turret. Because the use of *Upkeep* required close coordination between pilot, bomb-aimer, flight engineer and navigator, continuing the mission was out of the question. After a crew conference conducted with pencil and paper, Munro reluctantly turned back towards Scampton.

Another minute later 3./MF 246 engaged Vern Byers' 'K-for-King' (ED934) as it overflew nearby Texel Island. During the 62-minute DR leg across the sea, a stronger-than-forecast northerly wind had blown AJ–K three to five miles (5–8km) south of the planned route so that the aircraft approached the northern tip of Texel instead of the narrow neck of Vlieland. Byers climbed to 400–450ft apparently to give his navigator, Fg Off James Warner, opportunity to visually confirm their location and get his bearings. As AJ–K passed over the island and headed across the Waddenzee – the band of water between the Frisian Islands and the Dutch mainland – the aircraft was hit by a 105mm shell. Byers struggled to maintain control but AJ–K was seen to catch fire and crashed soon afterwards about 18 miles (29km) west of Harlingen. Byers and his six crew were all killed.

Flak was still peppering the air when 'H-for-Harry' roared across the narrow neck of Vlieland. Right on course, Geoff Rice flew so low he had to climb to skim over the island's sand dunes. Once across Vlieland he climbed a bit to confirm position, then descended once more and headed towards Stavoren – a small town on a prominent cape along the eastern shore of the IJsselmeer. As Rice flew into the 'gloomy moonlight' the haze obscured the dark horizon and the heavy Lancaster gradually sank through the night air. Just at the moment when flight engineer Sgt Edward Smith noticed that the barometric altimeter read zero, a tremendous jolt shuddered through the aircraft as it skipped off the glassy-smooth sea. Instinctively Rice pulled up, feeling a second 'violent jolt' as the *Upkeep* was torn away and smashed into the tailwheel, driving it up through the main spar of the horizontal stabilizer. Rear gunner Sgt Steve Burns shouted 'Christ! It's wet at the back ...', then: 'You've lost the mine.' Indeed, 'H-for-Harry' had glanced off the water, causing the *Upkeep* to be wrenched from its braces. The aircraft scooped up a small tsunami that flooded through the rear fuselage, almost drowning Burns before it drained out of the rear turret. After recovering to normal flight and climbing away, Rice realised that without the *Upkeep*, continuing the mission was pointless, so he too returned to Scampton.

The only member of the diversionary force to make it through the first cordon of defence was 'E-for-Easy' (ED927), flown by Norm Barlow. After crossing 'feet-dry' at Harderwijk, Barlow angled towards Rees in Germany, then turned eastwards to avoid the heavily defended Ruhr. At this point, just after rolling out of the turn, in the inky blackness of the night the big, low-flying Lancaster clipped the top of a steel pylon carrying high-tension electricity lines. The thundering bomber staggered and shed parts as showers of sparks arced across the darkness, torching the aircraft's fuel tanks. At 2350 the flaming Lancaster crashed spectacularly into a broad farmer's field three miles (4.8km) northeast of Rees. All aboard were killed.

Meanwhile, flying at 200mph (322km/hr), McCarthy drove 'T-for-Tommy' hard across the North Sea, making up 13 minutes by the time he overflew Vlieland. MF 246's 20mm gun crews were still alert and opened fire, forcing the American pilot to dive between 'two large sand dunes right on the coast' to spoil their aim.

As AJ–T bored across the IJsselmeer, another threat appeared. Three minutes after 3./MF 246 reported engaging the first low-flying Lancaster, Munro's AJ–W – and most probably in response to it – IV. *Gruppe/Nachtjagdgeschwader* 1 (4th Group/Nightfighter Wing 1, or IV./NJG 1) scrambled several Messerschmitt Bf 110G nightfighters from *Fliegerhorst* Leeuwaarden, east of the IJsselmeer. These climbed to the normal *Nachtjagd* operating altitudes of 3,280–19,685ft (1,000–6,000m) and flew across the IJsselmeer to patrol above the Helder peninsula (*Zone Hering*). As they passed overhead McCarthy reported he 'could quite frequently see [the Luftwaffe nightfighters] flying along at 1,000 feet above us'.

The 22 Bf 110G-4a aircraft of IV./NJG 1 were equipped with the rudimentary Telefunken *Funk-Gerät* 202 *Lichtenstein* B/C radar. Because of the radar's limited range (less than 4km/2.5 miles), the aircrew needed ground intercept controllers' vectors to place the fighter within its 'intercept volume'.

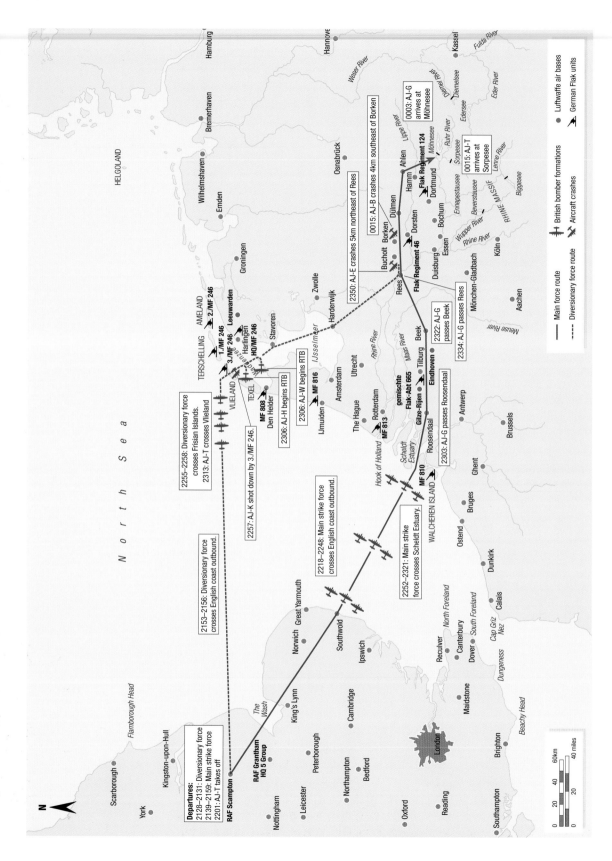

Departures:
2128–2131: Diversionary force takes off
2139–2159: Main strike force
2201: AJ-T takes off

RAF Scampton

RAF Grantham
HQ 5 Group

2153–2156: Diversionary force crosses English coast outbound.

2218–2248: Main strike force crosses English coast outbound.

2252–2321: Main strike force crosses Scheldt Estuary.

2303: AJ-G passes Roosendaal

2334: AJ-G passes Rees

2322: AJ-G passes Beek

2255–2258: Diversionary force crosses Frisian Islands.
2313: AJ-T crosses Vlieland

2257: AJ-K shot down by 3./MF 246.

2306: AJ-H begins RTB

2306: AJ-W begins RTB

2350: AJ-E crashes 5km northeast of Rees

0015: AJ-B crashes 4km southeast of Borken

0003: AJ-G arrives at Möhnesee

0015: AJ-T arrives at Sorpesee

MF 808

MF 813

MF 810

MF 816

HQ/MF 246

1./MF 246

2./MF 246

3./MF 246

Flak-Abt 665
gemischte

Flak-Regiment 46

Flak-Regiment 124

North Sea

Legend:
— Main force route
- - - Diversionary force route
• Luftwaffe air bases
🛩 German Flak units
✈ British bomber formations
✈ Aircraft crashes

However, below 1,000m (3,280ft) the three 'scopes' (azimuth, elevation and range) would 'cloud over as a result of ground returns' and therefore required a clear ('look-up') background if the target was to be visible. During Operation *Chastise* the 617 Sqn pilots flew their Lancasters beneath both the *Himmelbett* controllers' Würzburg radar screens and the nightfighters' patrol altitudes and, therefore, below the latters' on-board radar.

After a fruitless 105-minute flight at least one of these, from 12. *Staffel*/NJG 1 and crewed by *Feldwebel* (Sgt) Georg Kraft and *Feldwebel* Erich Handke, landed at *Fliegerhorst* Bergen, near Alkmaar in north Holland, to refuel. Later they would have another chance to intercept a 617 Sqn Lancaster, during the Dambusters' egress back through the Netherlands.

Main force departs: 2139–2159

While the diversionary force was making its individual takeoffs, the nine Lancasters of the main strike force taxied to the south end of Scampton's large grass field. Eight minutes after Rice's departure, Gibson swung 'G-for-George' into the wind, with 'Mick' Martin (AJ–P) on his left wing and 'Hoppy' Hopgood (AJ–M) on his right. A dozen Merlins roared and the three bombers accelerated slowly across the field, lifting their tails into the air. Climbing out laboriously, barely clearing the trees lining the northern edge of the aerodrome, Gibson banked left to circle back overhead Scampton, pointing southeast across the Wash and East Anglia.

Flying at 100ft (30.5m) or less in the waning light, Gibson led his section the 97 miles (156km) across the southwest corner of the North Sea, the enemy coast appearing in the gloom about two minutes behind schedule. However, the 34 minutes over water resulted in a slight drift and the formation made landfall southwest of the intended turn point (51° 38´N/03° 40´E), crossing Walcheren Island in doing so. Gibson climbed to 300ft (91.5m) to help his navigator, Plt Off 'Terry' Taerum, re-orient himself and Taerum quickly calculated a revised heading to the next turn point.

By this time darkness had enveloped the Netherlands, but a 'ghostly full moon' beamed from the 'perfectly clear' night sky to the southeast. In spite of the moon's full illumination, as Gibson turned hard left to correct course, Hopgood reportedly lost sight of his leader. However, his navigator, Fg Off Ken Earnshaw, RCAF, kept 'M-Mother' more or less on course for the Möhnesee after that.

Flying almost due east, Gibson skirted south of the Gilze-Rijen *Nachtjagd* base and just east of Tilburg picked up the Wilhelmina Canal, the water reflecting moonlight and marking a bright path across the dark ground. Following this prominent feature kept them north of Eindhoven, the other *Nachtjagd* base.

At a tiny town called Beek the Wilhelmina Canal ended abruptly in a distinctive T-intersection with the Zuid-Willemsvaartkanaal. From there, Gibson angled east-northeast across the flat, almost featureless terrain of North Brabant. Again Gibson drifted south of course. The broad undulating silver ribbon of the Rhine appeared out of the darkness ahead. At this point Gibson was looking for the two large bends in the river bracketing the small

MAY 14–15
1943

Final pre-strike photo reconnaissance of Ruhr dams

MAY 14
1943

No 617 Sqn conducts near-full-scale 'dress rehearsal' exercise.

German town of Rees. Realising he was some six miles (9.7km) south of the turn point, Gibson banked left to correct, flying across the turn point before banking back hard to the right to head east again, apparently slinging Martin's 'P-for-Popsie' from his left wing as he did so.

Near Rees the three leading Lancasters, now all flying individually, received their first hostile welcome: tracer shot into the night sky from flak positions along the riverbanks. The British turret gunners responded in kind, laying down suppressing fire with streams of all-tracer .303 machine-gun rounds until the Luftwaffe guns were left far behind. Further concentrations of enemy AA guns – belonging to *Flak-Regiment* 46 ('*Flakgruppe Dorsten*'), with four heavy and two light battalions – were encountered in the Bucholt-Borken area northwest of Dorsten and again near Dülmen.

Passing the latter, 20mm fire (most likely from *Leichte Flak-Abteilung* 881) raked Hopgood's 'M-for-Mother', wounding front gunner Plt Off George Gregory and wireless operator Sgt John Minchin and damaging the number-one (port-outer) engine. Some time later, flight engineer Sgt Charles Brennan shut down the ailing Merlin and feathered the propeller, pushing up the other three throttles to maintain planned airspeed.

Just northeast of Hamm Gibson spotted the final turn point – the intersection of several railway lines at the northeast edge of Ahlen – and banked right to a southerly heading, flying between Soest and Werl. Gibson admitted to being off course several times *en route*, and he may have been so at this point. Whereas Taerum's logbook shows the aircraft arriving at the Möhne at 0003 (three minutes after TOT), most histories have AJ–G arriving at 0015, well after Martin had shown up.[1]

Young's formation, having experienced similar navigational errors and abrupt corrections, lost Shannon (most likely slung from the left wing during the hard right turn at Rees) and passed through flak just past Dülmen and near Ahlen. The pair arrived in the target area at 0026, followed shortly by Shannon.

Meanwhile, at about 0012 Maudslay's section made the turn at Rees and headed east. Fg Off Harold Hobday insisted on 'strict individual navigation' among this section and, passing an intermediate checkpoint, Maudslay and Knight made a slight turn that Astell seemed 'uncertain of', perhaps due to the last-minute change in ingress routing to avoid Hüls.

This hesitation – resulting in an 'S'-turn to be sure of their position and proper direction – placed 'B-for-Baker' about one minute (about three miles/5km) behind the other two, on the same track towards Ahlen. At 0015, just south of Borken, the Lancaster struck the top of a steel electricity pylon, bringing down the pylon's upper section and two cables. Witnesses on the ground saw sparks shower across the sky as the big bomber reared up and then staggered into a descent. It barely cleared a large farmhouse before

---

1 While all publications on the Dams Raid give Gibson's arrival time as 0015, this likely results from misreading Taerum's logbook. Adding the *en route* times for each leg sequentially to the takeoff time of 2139 results in an arrival time at the Möhne Dam at 0003. The erroneous '0015' arrival time may come from the well used photocopy of Taerum's logbook page, the last line of which reads: 'Target A ... 114½, 110, 6°W, 116, 181, 46, 15¼', and interpreting the entry in the 'time' column (15¼) as being the ATA (actual time of arrival) at Möhne when it is actually the ATE (actual time *en route*) from the Möhne to the Eder Dam.

crashing into a large field 650ft (198m) beyond, erupting into a huge fireball on impact. The *Upkeep* weapon was seen to roll from the flames – which had also touched off a spectacular fireworks display of exploding tracer ammunition – a distance of about 500ft (152m). Then it exploded with a huge blast, leaving a crater 'as big as a house'. None of the aircrew survived.

By 0032 the main and diversionary forces – 14 bombers despatched – arrived in the target area. Two Lancasters had been lost to flak and two others in collisions with pylons, and another pair had aborted the mission – one due to flak damage and the other due to losing its weapon. A seventh bomber was badly damaged by flak, but arrived to carry out its attack anyway. Thus, on ingress alone, the *Chastise* strike forces had experienced 50% casualties (lost, damaged or aborted) before the first attack was even flown. The losses would not end there.

Main force attacks Möhne Dam: 0028–0049

The Möhne-Talsperre was defended by 3. *Batterie/Leichte Flak-Abteilung* 840, a subordinate unit of *Flak-Regiment* 124 ('*Flakgruppe Dortmund*'), commanded by a Leutnant Widmann. The unit was equipped with six single-barrelled, optically sighted and manually trained 20mm *Flak* 38 (*Fliegerabwehrkanone* 38) automatic cannon. Of these, two were positioned atop the sluice towers, one on the 'overlook balcony' on the northern wing of the dam, and the other three below the dam, along the north side of the compensating basin protecting the electricity-generating powerplant.

The Rheinmetall *Flak* 38 was an extremely effective light AA gun, firing 4oz (113g) armour-piercing and high-explosive shells at a rate of about 200 rounds per minute. Against airborne targets it had a maximum effective range of 7,218ft (2,200m), but doctrine dictated opening fire at approximately 3,280ft (1,000m), using open sights for the first burst and the flight of tracers to correct to the target.

As his aircraft arrived over the Möhnesee, wireless operator Flt Lt Robert 'Hutch' Hutchison, DFC, switched on the VHF and Gibson called for a 'check-in' of his section. 'Cooler 2' and 'Cooler 3' answered and the mission commander said: 'Stand by, chaps, I'm going to look the place over'. At 0023 (according to 3./le Flak-Abt. 840) Gibson made one dummy run reconnoitring the target and its defences, then announced: 'I like the look of it'.

According to one historian (and this is repeated by others), the 'agreed tactic' originated at the Köbecke bridge located on the main branch of the Möhnesee. However, there is no substantiation of this in the archives and while it may have been discussed during the briefing, Gibson after making his dummy run apparently favoured using the Torhaus bridge spanning the *Hevearm des Möhnesees* (the Heve branch of the Möhne lake) as the IP. He crossed this westbound and then turned right onto a course of 330° (magnetic) so as to point at the dam. He later wrote: 'Straightening up we began to dive [across the Heversberg] towards the flat, ominous water two miles away [the 'agreed tactic' would have arrived on track only 1,640yd (1500m) from the dam]. Over the front turret was the dam silhouetted against the haze of the Ruhr Valley.' The fact that he dived across the

THE MÖHNE DAM

17 MAY 1943

Objective: To breach the Möhne dam from the lake side by using the weapons delivery profile developed for the *Upkeep* anti-dam weapon. The attack profile was complicated somewhat by the moderately high terrain of the Heversberg (262m elevation; 50m above the lake) jutting into the lake approximately 1,900 yards/1,740 meters from the dam. Crossing this, the bombers had to descend rapidly in order to achieve the required 60ft *Upkeep* release height with enough time to stabilize other parameters before arriving at the release point.

N

GÜNNE VI

MÖHNE RIVER

MÖHNE DAM

HEVERSBERG

▼ ACTIONS

1 The pilot positioned the aircraft over east end of the shallow valley of the Hevesee and approached on a westerly heading to cross the Torhaus Bridge (IP).

2 Approaching the 'run-in' course, the pilot turned right to aim at the centre of the dam, flying across a crest of the Heversberg at minimum height.

3 The pilot descended to and maintained a 60ft height of above the lake surface cuing off the navigator's 'high'/'low'/'steady' calls based on the two 'altimeter spotlights'.

4 The flight engineer adjusted the throttles to prevent acceleration in the descent and maintain the prescribed 220mph during the approach 'run in'.

5 If the above parameters were met, the bomb-aimer released *Upkeep* 450 yards /412 meters from the dam based on use of his triangulation bombsight.

6 Upon release, *Upkeep* would skip across the lake surface three times and strike the 'water side' of the dam, roll down the dam wall and detonate at 30ft depth.

7 Upon weapon release – or passing over the dam – the pilot called for maximum power and pulled up, banking to the left to return to the IP if *Upkeep* had not been released, or to view the results of the attack if it had.

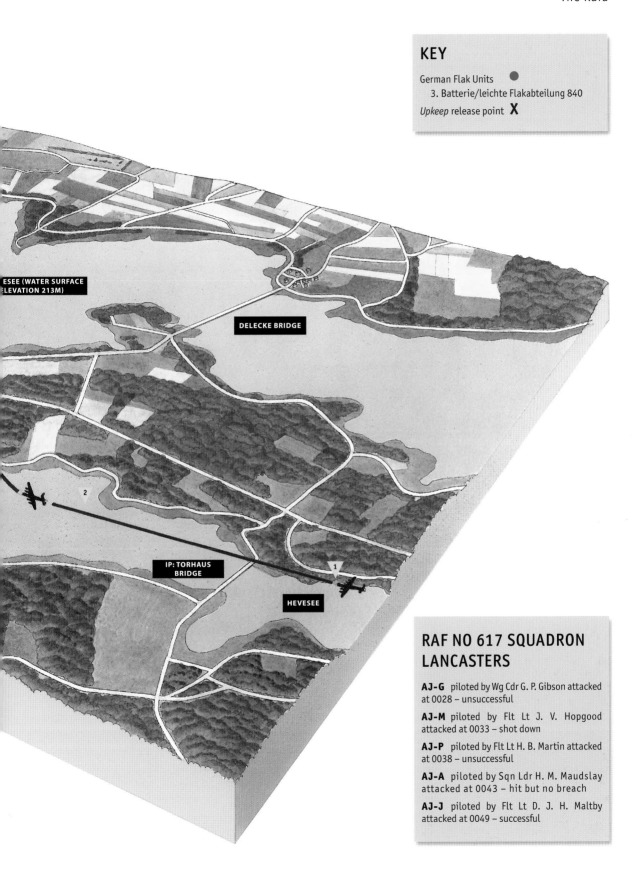

KEY

German Flak Units ●
  3. Batterie/leichte Flakabteilung 840
Upkeep release point **X**

ESEE (WATER SURFACE ELEVATION 213M)

DELECKE BRIDGE

IP: TORHAUS BRIDGE

HEVESEE

RAF NO 617 SQUADRON LANCASTERS

AJ-G piloted by Wg Cdr G. P. Gibson attacked at 0028 – unsuccessful

AJ-M piloted by Flt Lt J. V. Hopgood attacked at 0033 – shot down

AJ-P piloted by Flt Lt H. B. Martin attacked at 0038 – unsuccessful

AJ-A piloted by Sqn Ldr H. M. Maudslay attacked at 0043 – hit but no breach

AJ-J piloted by Flt Lt D. J. H. Maltby attacked at 0049 – successful

Heversberg is confirmed by bomb-aimer Plt Off Frederick 'Spam' Spafford, DFM, RAAF, warning Gibson: 'You're going to hit those trees!'

Posterity is indebted to Arthur G. Thorning – an aeronautical engineer as well as a pilot and historian – for the scientific analysis of the Dambusters' Möhne attack profile. Descending from across the Heversberg to gain the necessary 220mph (355km/h), Gibson arrived at 60ft (18m) about 1,650yd (1,509m) from the dam, giving himself, flight engineer Sgt John Pulford and Spafford 11 seconds to achieve the parameters before the release point.

Alerted by the dummy run, the crews of the six flak guns manned their weapons and opened up on the approaching bomber. The crews later reported sustained attacks from 0030–0045. One gun captain, *Unteroffizier* (Corporal) Karl Schütte, later reported: 'Suddenly we saw one aircraft send out two powerful beams of light on the lake as it hurtled low towards the middle of the dam wall. By doing this they gave us a good marker as to their position and we no longer needed to aim towards the sound or the shadow.'

In the face of steady streams of 20mm tracer lancing out from the three flak guns atop the dam wall, F/Sgt Andrew Deering clattered away with his twin rifle-calibre Brownings from the front turret.

In the event, Gibson must have had a slight left bank on 'G-for-George' at the moment Spafford pressed the release button, 'Spam' having called for left corrections in the last seconds. The *Upkeep* bounced three times, veered off to the left and, according to German reports, was stopped before the western sluice tower by the torpedo nets (buoyed 27.3yd/25m and 33.9yd/31m from the dam wall), then sank and exploded, causing a dark, muddy geyser to drench Lt Widmann's four-man *Flak* 38 crew.

Gibson circled the dam, keeping a safe distance from the flak guns, as his crew waited anxiously for the dam to crack and rupture, but it did not. At 0037 Hutchison tapped out in Morse: 'Goner 68A' – signifying that the *Upkeep* had been released but exploded 5–50yd from the Möhne dam with no breach in the structure. After waiting for the lake surface to return to a glassy calm, Gibson called Hopgood. 'Cooler 2, it's your turn to attack. It's a piece of cake.'[2]

'O.K. Cooler 2, attacking.'

Hopgood flew the same profile. Gibson reported that AJ–M went 'down over the trees where I had come from a few moments before', arriving at attack height well before the release point. However, by this time the flak gunners had found the proper elevation and range.

Uffz Schütte described 'Cooler 2's' approach: 'It came roaring at us out of the moonlight like a monster, as if it wanted to ram us on the tower – but we didn't think about the danger … We fired for all we were worth … and then I clearly saw the streams of tracer drumming into the aircraft, and moments later a flame billowed out. "It's burning! It's burning!" I yelled to my men, as the aircraft rushed past us, trailing a sheet of flame.'

---

2 While almost all previous histories use the 'AJ + letter' identifier as the reference employed in Gibson and others' VHF transmissions, this appears to result from the fact that this information was unclassified and released for use, while for many years afterwards the individual 'Cooler' callsigns were not. The 'AJ'-series identifiers were used for Morse-code communications (W/T over HF radios), while 'Cooler' callsigns were more common with voice R/T over VHF radios. Given his fighter experience Gibson most probably used the 'Cooler' callsigns to direct the attacks and conduct conversations; hence these are used here.

Indeed, 'M-for-Mother' had been mortally wounded in the exchange. Passing the release point, the number-two (port-inner) Merlin was hit and caught fire, and the starboard 'inboard petrol tanks [erupted into] a long jet of flame'. The bomb-aimer, F/Sgt John Fraser, RCAF, was not satisfied with the release parameters and aborted the drop, but when he saw how the aeroplane had been so critically damaged he released the weapon anyway, as much to lighten the load as attempt any damage.

The *Upkeep* skipped just once and then hurtled over the dam, crashing into the power station below. Ninety seconds later it exploded, demolishing the building along with the turbines and transformers inside, and sending a pall of thick smoke and steam curling into the air.

The blast blew two of Widmann's guncrew from their perch atop the western sluice tower, although they were not injured, and knocked the *Flak 38* from its base. His gun out of action, Widmann sent his remaining ammunition over to Schütte's crew while they swapped the overheated barrels and oiled up their weapons, just in time for the next attack.

Meanwhile, the stricken 'M-for-Mother' cleared the dam and clawed for altitude. Flight engineer Brennan tried to extinguish the engine fire. However, he could not, and he told everyone to prepare to bale out. Hopgood, only 25 seconds after passing the dam – once he had got the doomed bomber to 500ft (142m) – ordered the crew to abandon the aircraft. Fraser needed no further prompting and tumbled through the forward escape hatch.

The rear gunner, Plt Off Tony Burcher, RAAF, scrambled from his rear turret, opened the aft crew door and plugged into the intercom in time to hear Hopgood saying: 'If only I had another 300 feet – I can't get any more height … for Christ's sake get out of here!'

The wireless operator, Minchin, who had been badly wounded, crawled to the aft crew door too but was too weak to continue. Burcher pulled Minchin's D-ring and shoved him out, but the wireless operator did not survive. Almost immediately afterwards, as Burcher stood in the doorway, the starboard tanks exploded, folding the wing and catapulting him from the blazing aircraft.

The starboard wing separated and 'M-for-Mother' (ED925) crashed in a shower of flaming debris 3.7 miles (6km) beyond the dam, between the villages of Sieveringen and Ostönnen. The wreck continued to burn furiously during the remaining attacks.

Burcher had managed to deploy his parachute, but was injured – his back was broken, probably from hitting the tailplane – and he was captured soon after landing. Fraser landed in a wheatfield. He escaped the initial manhunt and the next night slipped through the cordon, headed for Holland. However, ten days later and only 30 miles (48km) from the border he was captured. He would be held in a series of prisoner-of-war camps – including the famous *Stalag-Luft* III, where he played a role in the 'Great Escape'.

Now, at 0038, 'Cooler 3' descended down the north slope of the Heversberg to the *Upkeep* delivery height. Learning from Hopgood's loss, Gibson flew ahead and high on Martin's starboard side, switching on his altimeter spotlights so as to distract the enemy gunners while Deering sprayed the remaining flak positions with his machine-guns.

Overleaf
Aiming Lancaster AJ-J at the centre of the Möhne Dam, Flt Lt David Maltby cleared the thickly wooded Heversberg and descended to 60ft above the Möhnesee. As the two 'altimeter spotlight' circles merged into a 'figure 8', navigator Sgt Vivian Nicholson called 'steady… steady…', and Maltby held the big bomber level while flight engineer Sgt William Hatton adjusted the throttles to reach the prescribed speed of 220mph (354 km/hr). In the front turret, Sgt Victor Hill opened fire with his two Browning machine guns, duelling with one of the four German 20mm Flak 38s mounted along the dam wall. Below him in the nose, bomb-aimer Plt Off John Fort peered through his Dann bombsight, waiting for the two rapidly separating sluice towers to touch the white dowels of the rudimentary aiming device. At that point – 450 yards from the dam – Fort pressed the bomb release button and the backspinning *Upkeep* dropped from the Lancaster and skipped over the lake's surface towards its target. High and to the left Flt Lt "Mick" Martin piloted AJ-P across the west end of the dam, his navigation lights glowing and his gunners firing to draw enemy fire. Wg Cdr Guy Gibson flew AJ-G across the east end of the dam, doing the same. while the wreckage of Flt Lt John Hopgood's AJ-M burned fiercely in the distance.

Schütte recounts: 'The sound of engines swelled again after the smoke dispersed. The swooping aircraft once again turned on their lamps, enabling us to focus on them. We opened fire – which the aircraft replied immediately. Now a third aircraft [AJ–P] came in a direct attack. We changed target on the incoming four-engined monster …' 'P-for-Popsie' was hit, but not badly – with an empty fuel tank holed.

Bob Hay succeeded in releasing his *Upkeep* at the right point, but Martin had apparently just added some left bank – probably attempting to correct from his 335° heading onto the proper course. The cylinder caught its left edge on the water and immediately curved dramatically into one of the narrow inlets on the dam's western end, then exploded to no effect.

At about 0052 wireless operator Fg Off Leonard Chambers, RNZAF, tapped out: 'Goner 58A' – signifying that the *Upkeep* had been released and exploded 50–100yd from the Möhne dam with no breach in the structure.

'Once the mirror of the lake had settled again, the fourth aircraft came in on the attack,' Schütte reported. 'But we no longer knew which aircraft we should engage first, as the four-engine monsters were flying in together in the attack.'

At 0043 'Cooler 4' began its approach, aimed at the centre of the Möhne Dam. Meanwhile Gibson orbited to the northern side, flying parallel to the dam to allow both front and rear gunners to stream tracers down at the two remaining flak positions. He recounted: 'We stayed at a fairly safe distance on the other side, firing with all guns at the defences, and the defences, like the stooges they were, firing back at us. We were both out of range of each other, but the ruse seemed to work.' Martin flew in with Young, high and to the left, Martin's front-gunner Plt Off Gordon Yeo also pouring streams of .303 tracer at the dam's defences.

Young carried out a textbook run-in – just as Wallis had prescribed – and his bomb-aimer, Fg Off Vincent MacCausland, RCAF, released the *Upkeep* at the correct range. The weapon bounced three times, bounded straight into the wall and after impact sank beside it. Schütte said: 'Then a big explosion and an amazing column of water. Once more the Möhne Lake shook, and once again, great waves beat against the crown of the dam … Luckily the wall stood still after the fourth attack.'

At 0050 Young's wireless operator, Sgt Larry Nichols, sent: 'Goner 78A', signifying that the *Upkeep* had been released and exploded in contact with the Möhne Dam, but with no breach in the structure.

Once again allowing the waters to subside – and the great cloud of mist caused by the geyser to dissipate – Gibson called on 'Cooler 5' to make his run at the mighty Möhne.

But by this time Schütte's *Flak* 38 had experienced a premature shell detonation in the barrel that jammed the weapon. 'So we stood on the tower. In front of us was the lake and behind us the valley – but we couldn't fight back any more … Then the fifth bomber came in on the attack and flew in over the middle of the dam with furious speed – it was child's play for him now … But our guns were silent. And now we did what we had practised so often, attacking the aircraft with carbines out of pure self-defence.'

Now, Gibson and Martin were orbiting the dam – to the east and west respectively – with their gunners pouring tracer streams down upon the flak positions. At 0049 David Maltby also made a textbook attack: on a course of 330° aimed at the centre of the dam and at an airspeed of 223mph (359km/hr). The bomb-aimer, Plt Off John Fort, released the *Upkeep* at the prescribed range.

But even as Maltby's *Upkeep* bounded towards the aim point, he saw the hoped-for result beginning to happen right before his eyes: 'The crown of the wall was already crumbling … [there was] a tremendous amount of debris on top'.

However, the full effect was not yet evident. At 0050 his wireless operator, Sgt A. J. Stone, sent another disappointing 'Goner 78A' to 5 Group HQ at Grantham.

Nevertheless, there was another huge, misty eruption. Gibson 'watched for about five minutes, and it was rather hard to see anything, for now the air was full of spray from these explosions … so I called up Dave Shannon and told him to come in. As he turned I got close to the dam wall and then saw what happened. It had rolled over, but I could not believe my eyes … There was no doubt about it – there was a great breach 100 yards across, and the water, looking like stirred porridge in the moonlight was gushing out and rolling into the Ruhr Valley towards the industrial centres of Germany's Third Reich.'

Calling for 'Cooler 6' to abort his attack, Gibson circled the dam – his crew and the others gathering amazed at the sight before them – and at 0056 directed 'Hutch' to signal 'Nigger' – signifying 'Möhne breached; diverting to Eder'.

After taking three more minutes to appreciate the dramatic result of their efforts, Gibson organised the next phase of the operation. He sent Martin and Maltby home (AJ–J had departed the target area at 0053.5, beginning the return to base, or RTB) and directed the remaining 'Cooler' aircraft to head to Target 'B'.

Back at Grantham, in 5 Group's underground operations centre, Cochrane, Satterly and Wallis were joined by ACM Harris, monitoring 617 Sqn's attacks through Wg Cdr Dunn, who sat at the end of a long conference table listening for the Morse-code reports on a telephone handset. Opposite the table the night's RAF and WAAF duty staff gradually filled in the operations chalkboard as progress reports were received from 'Cooler' aircraft.

Tensions were high – and anxiety and apprehension mounting – as the first few 'Goner' reports were relayed by Dunn. Because 'Cooler 4' reported ahead of Gibson's wingmen, it was feared that Martin as well as Hopgood had been brought down in the attacks. Three near-simultaneous 'no-breach' reports made Wallis lose confidence in his creation. He put his head in his hands, saying 'No, it's no good'.

Three minutes later Gibson's 'Möhne breached' message came through and elation erupted throughout the room. Wallis leapt into the air and pumped his arms vigorously. Even the stern 'Butch' Harris grinned and congratulated the engineer.

While Gibson led Young, Maudslay, Shannon and Knight to the Eder, the 5 Group staff began to consider target assignments for the reserve force.

MAY 15 1943

No 617 Sqn makes final preparations for *Chastise*

MAY 16 1943

2128–2131 Diversionary force departs RAF Scampton

'T-for-Tommy' attacks the Sorpe Dam: 0046

'T-for-Tommy' arrived at the Sorpesee at 0015. During the inbound flight the aircraft had sustained some damage – a punctured starboard main-gear tyre – from light AA guns mounted on a train, probably belonging to *Flak-Regiment* 112 (*Eisenbahn*). Joe McCarthy, surprised that there was no evidence of attacks by the other members of his formation, positioned his big bomber over the village of Langscheid for the first attack.

High above the silent hilltop village – clearly visible in the bright moonlight – McCarthy looked down on the narrow throat of the Sorpe valley, spanned by an earthen dam 2,100ft (640m) long. He blurted out: 'Jeez! How do we get down there?'

Ordering Radcliffe to lower flaps to 20° and reduce power to maintain 180mph (290km/h), McCarthy swung 'T-for-Tommy' around to align it with the extended line of the dam then dived down the hill as if on a rollercoaster, levelling out as low as possible. McCarthy lined up the number-one (port-outer) engine nacelle with the road along the top of the dam and flew as low as he dared. He and Radcliffe had only three seconds to stabilise the delivery parameters before passing the centre point of the dam. The hill at the other end of the dam loomed larger and larger. The bomb-aimer, F/Sgt George 'Johnny' Johnson, decided he was not satisfied and called 'dummy run', without releasing the *Upkeep*.

Calling for full power on the four Merlins, McCarthy pulled up sharply into a climb. Clearing the hill beyond he banked left and hauled his heavily laden Lancaster – straining from G-forces plus the effect of carrying nearly five tons of depth charge on its belly – around in a 'racetrack' pattern to arrive over Langscheid for another try. The aircraft dived and levelled off. With only seconds to judge the parameters and release point, Johnson once pronounced himself again dissatisfied. He repeated this on seven subsequent attack runs.

On the tenth try, at 0046, from an altitude of 30ft (9.1m) and with an airspeed of only 170mph (288km/h), Johnson finally released the *Upkeep* just past the centre point of the dam. The depth charge rolled off to the right and disappeared into the water. As soon as McCarthy felt the heavy *Upkeep* release, he pulled up sharply and called for maximum power, almost standing the big bomber on its tail. 'T-for-Tommy' soared upwards, nose pointed into the night sky, and sailed to 1,000ft (305m) altitude at an alarming rate. The rear gunner, Fg Off Dave Rodger, RCAF, quickly yelled: 'Get the hell down … [we're] a sitting duck at this height!'

At about this time Rodger saw a tremendous geyser of water shoot high into the air. He exclaimed 'God Almighty!'

McCarthy circled around to the left for several minutes, descending to a safe altitude for a closer look. The crew believed they saw some 'crumbling along the top of the dam', but Wallis' fears were confirmed: no breach occurred.

Vertical view of the Sorpe Dam and its surrounding area. The large hilltop village of Langscheid – over which Flt Lt McCarthy orbited so as to line up for the attack – can clearly be seen near the western end of the earthen dam (left). North is at top of the photo. (IWM Photo MH 3780)

After waiting about 15 minutes with nothing happening, McCarthy finally pointed 'T-for-Tommy' homeward. In the excitement of the moment the crew forgot to report the release of the *Upkeep* at the Sorpe or its results until 0300. As far as HQ 5 Group knew, none of the diversionary-force Lancasters had actually bombed the Sorpe.

Main force attacks Eder Dam: 0130–0152

The Ederstausee is a very long, wide, serpentine lake whose coils and cataracts are tightly compressed. In fact, immediately upstream of the dam the lake curls dramatically to the right before bending back sharply 180°. The length of the run-in would be severely limited if flown perpendicularly (approximately 120°M track) because the steep-sided, thickly-forested peninsula, called the Hammerberg, pointed into the centre of the 180° left turn only 1,000yd (915m) from the dam face. The Hammerberg formed a plateau some 330ft (100m) – counting tree height – above the surface of the water. Coupling the very short approach with an aggressive dive – which typically increased airspeed – resulted in only three or four seconds of level flight in which to make the final adjustments before weapon release.

These facts would have been obvious if the tabletop model of the target area had been provided for the mission briefing, but that important planning asset was not completed until the day after the raid. All the crews had to go on were RAF overhead reconnaissance photos. Estimates of terrain elevation based on these pictures were off by more than 125ft (38m).

Just before 0130, Gibson called 'Cooler 6' and directed Shannon to begin the attacks. The Australian executed the attack profile as briefed, descending from over Waldeck Castle more or less parallel to the dam, turning hard left to point between the two sluice towers and after crossing the Hammerberg, diving quickly to 60ft (18.3m), with the target rushing towards them. However, F/Sgt Leonard Sumpter was not satisfied with the parameters and did not release *Upkeep*.

Shannon later stated: 'To get out of the valley after crossing the dam wall we had to put on full throttle and do a steep climbing turn to avoid a vast rock face.' This was the Michelskopf – a sheer 1,380ft (420m) mass of stone just past the dam, standing directly on the 120° track beyond it. Circling around to the left, Shannon flew AJ–L back to Waldeck Castle to try it again.

After the third dummy run, Gibson told Shannon: 'OK, Dave, you hang around for a bit and I'll get another aircraft to have a crack … Hello, Cooler 7? You can go in now.'

Maudslay's luck was no better. After two unsuccessful attempts, Gibson directed Shannon to try again.

It is clear from the individual flight logs that frustration at being unable to achieve the desired release parameters while approaching on the proper attack axis motivated modifications to the briefed profile. It seems that Shannon, on his sixth pass of the night, decided to forgo crossing the high Hammerberg at all and approached the Eder-Talsperre on a course of 150°M, passing the end of the peninsula and aiming at the dam some 30° off

THE SORPE DAM

17 MAY 1943

Objective: Because the *Sorpetalsperre* was an earthen berm-type dam, *Upkeep* could not be employed as it was designed for a typical masonry dam. Rather than attack perpendicular to the dam, the attackers had to fly along the length of the dam and deposit it at the top of the 'water side' slope whereupon it would roll downhill into the lake. Upon detonation, it was hoped that the resulting 'pressure wave' through the earthen embankment would 'crack' the concrete core, allowing the subsequent underground leak to erode and weaken the structure sufficiently to cause its eventual collapse.

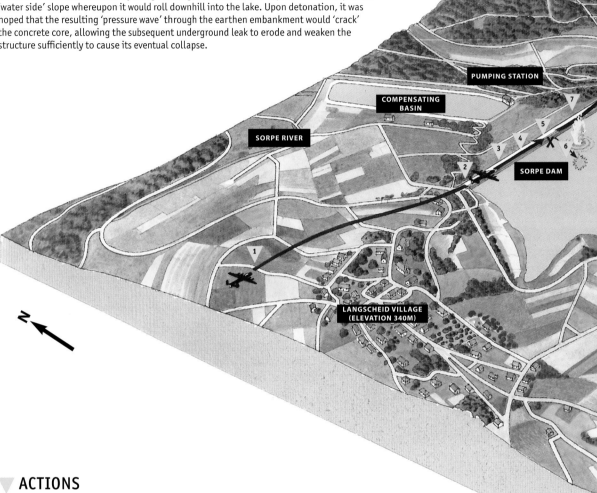

▼ ACTIONS

1 The pilot positioned his aircraft over the village of Langscheid (IP), just north and east of the church spire, and approached the dam from the northwest aligned with it. Landing flaps 20° and airspeed 180 mph, the pilot descended sharply down the hillside to the dam.

2 The pilot maintained alignment and lateral (right) offset by lining bomber's 'port outer' (number one) engine nacelle with the roadway atop the dam.

3 The pilot flew down to and maintained the 'lowest practicable height' of 30–60ft by his visual perception, with the help of the navigator.

4 The flight engineer adjusted the throttles to maintain the 'slowest possible speed' (180mph desired) with enough energy for an abrupt 'pull up' at the end of the 'bomb run' without entering an accelerated stall.

5 If the above parameters were met, the bomb-aimer released *Upkeep* 'just short of the centre point of the dam' based solely upon his visual estimation of that point.

6 Released without spinning, *Upkeep* would roll forward and downhill into the water, continuing to roll down the embankment slope before detonating at 30ft depth.

7 Upon weapon release – or when he could not stand it any longer – the pilot called for maximum power and pulled up sharply to clear the steeply rising terrain of Hill 321.

8 Upon clearing Hill 321, the pilot would bank to the left and orbit back to Langscheid if *Upkeep* had not been released, or to view the results of the attack if it had.

HILL 321

8

SORPESEE (WATER SURFACE ELEVATION 283M)

KEY

Intended impact point **X**

RAF NO 617 SQUADRON LANCASTERS

ED825/AJ-T piloted by Flt Lt J. C. McCarthy attacked at 0046 – unsuccessful

ED918/AJ-F piloted by Flt Sgt K. W. Brown attacked at 0314 – unsuccessful

the intended track. This way it proved much easier to attain the proper release parameters. At 0139 Sumpter released *Upkeep*.

The depth-charge bounced only twice – indicating that it might have been dropped too close to the dam – and as Shannon pulled up sharply and banked right, Sgt Robert Henderson shoved the throttles 'through the gate' so as to clear the Michelskopf.

Behind them, the *Upkeep* struck the curved dam wall at an oblique angle (about 33°) and with excessive velocity. The weapon then ricocheted off to the right, unspent velocity coupled with residual backspin sending it careering into the shallow water near the dam's south end. There it exploded, sending up a huge geyser of mud and water that, according to German accounts, went 'mostly up into the air' but did damage the parapet, stairs and boat landing.

Fg Off Brian Goodale's signalled 'Goner 78C' – signifying that the *Upkeep* had been released and had exploded in contact with the Eder dam, causing a small breach in the structure. However, this was optimistic; despite this and Shannon's subsequent claims, Gibson, who had been shadowing each attack from high on the right side, gave the official verdict that 'no result was seen'.

Gibson then called Maudslay in for another try. It is not known whether Maudslay attempted the briefed attack profile or a modification of it. In any event, *Upkeep* was released too late, with too great an airspeed, or both. At 0146 the depth charge bounced once and hit the parapet, exploding on contact. 'Cooler 7' roared past, banking steeply to the right and pulling up to clear the Michelskopf.

'Z-for-Zebra' may have been damaged by the blast because Maudslay immediately headed back to the Möhne to join the planned return routes. Ten minutes later the wireless operator, Warrant Officer Alden Cottam, transmitted 'Goner 28B' – indicating that the *Upkeep* had been released and overshot the Eder Dam with no apparent breach.

Gibson now called upon the last remaining Lancaster in the main strike force, putting his trust in Plt Off Les Knight, RAAF, and the crew of 'N-for-Nuts'. His trust proved well founded.

Starting down the valley just north of Waldeck Castle, Knight adjusted his approach course. He flew across the Hammerberg somewhat east of the perpendicular approach line, where the terrain was lower (about 85ft/25m) and the distance to the dam was greater (about 600ft/180m). This meant Knight had less altitude to lose and an additional two seconds to do this in, which gave him and his crew more time to stabilise the parameters before reaching the *Upkeep* release point.

Even with Knight's modified approach, proper airspeed proved to be the hardest to attain. The flight engineer, Sgt Ray Grayston, reported: 'We carried out our first run, and [at 240mph] we were above the airspeed permitted, so we aborted the first run, but we learned a lot from it … so on the second run I choked the throttles right back to engine idle and let it [the aeroplane] glide down to the right height. There were only a few seconds involved here before you get level then release – five or seven seconds. As luck would have it, we flattened her out, got the speed right, all the rest doing their job, calling the airspeed, looking at the [altimeter] lights and calling high or low, and we were spot on, released the mine and blew the bottom out of the Eder Dam.'

Wireless operator F/Sgt Robert Kellow added: 'After the mine had dropped, Les pulled the nose up quite steeply in order to clear the hill, and in doing so, I could look back and down at the dam wall. It was still intact for a short while, then as if some huge fist had been jabbed at the wall, a large, almost round black hole appeared and the water gushed as from a large hose.'

The four crews circled the Eder as it continued to crumble, elated at their success. There was much 'whooping and hollering' over the VHF, with excited shouts of joy and hearty congratulations. After watching the torrent rage downstream, flooding the Eder valley, Gibson finally called: 'Good show, boys, let's all go home and get pie.'

At 0152, Hutchison tapped out 'Dinghy' to 5 Group HQ. Having heard nothing from the diversionary force, at 0210 Grantham asked 'Cooler 1' how many first-wave aircraft were available to attack Target 'Z'. Gibson's terse reply – 'none' – meant they must now coordinate the destruction of the Sorpe using the last few Lancasters now winging their way across the Rhine: the reserve force.

Reserve force launches: 0009–0300

Just as the main strike force began arriving at the Möhnesee and two badly damaged bombers (AJ–H and AJ–W) were approaching the English coastline on their premature returns to Scampton, the five crews of the reserve force climbed aboard their Lancasters, started the 20 Merlins and taxied out for take-off. The plan was to depart in the same manner used by the diversionary force – individual take-offs one minute apart – but to take the same route as the main strike force. Plt Off Warner Ottley, DFC, led off in AJ–C at 0009. He was followed by Plt Off Lewis Burpee, DFM, RCAF (AJ–S) and the three NCO pilots, with F/Sgt Cyril Anderson (AJ–Y) bringing up the rear at 0015.

By this time it was pitch dark, so aircrew could not see an aircraft ahead of them. Moreover, the moon was now past its zenith, reducing the amount of reflective illumination off waterways on the route and causing a corresponding loss of precision in navigation. F/Sgt Ken Brown (flying AJ–F) arrived at the Dutch coast a minute behind Burpee, at 0130, but was well off track – a problem most likely caused by a 5° error in the aircraft's compass. Getting back on some semblance of the correct course required a hard left turn, followed shortly by a reversal to the right.

Burpee – and his navigator, Sgt Thomas Jaye – may have also had difficulty in finding the way after making landfall. 'S-for-Sugar' strayed north, past Roosendaal. Ahead in the dark lay the large Luftwaffe *Nachtjagd* base of Gilze-Rijen. A Dutch army airfield taken over and much expanded by the Germans, Gilze-Rijen was home to nine radar-equipped Messerschmitt Bf 110G nightfighters of 1. *Staffel*/NJG 1 and seven Junkers Ju-88Cs of 10./NJG 3. *Fliegerhorst* Gilze-Rijen was defended by *gemischte Flak-Abteilung* 665, with four batteries of heavy AA guns – the famous,

THE EDER DAM

17 MAY 1943

Objective: To breach the Eder dam from the lake side by using the weapons delivery profile developed for the *Upkeep* anti-dam weapon. At the Eder, the attack profile was complicated by the high terrain of the Hammerberg (325m elevation; 100m above the lake surface including trees) jutting into the lake only 1,000 yards/915 meters from the back side of the dam. To be successful the attack profile had to be modified to an offset approach angle.

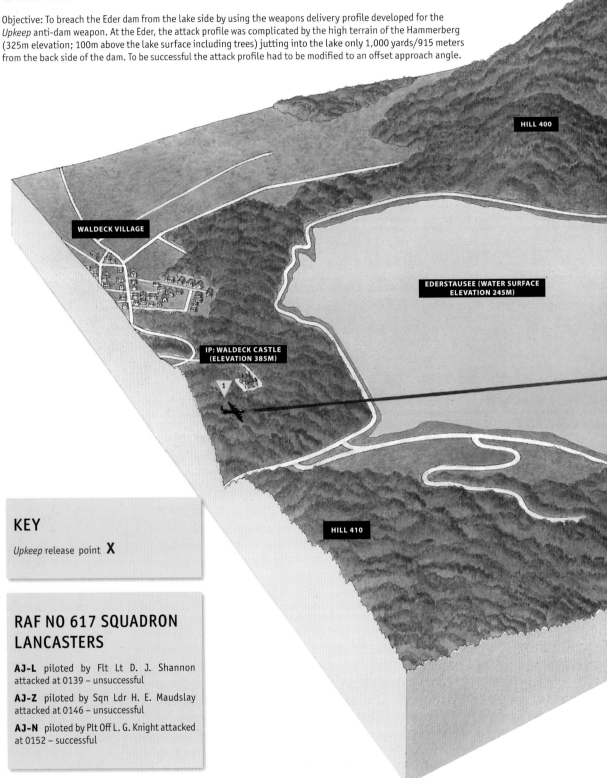

HILL 400

WALDECK VILLAGE

EDERSTAUSEE (WATER SURFACE ELEVATION 245M)

IP: WALDECK CASTLE (ELEVATION 385M)

HILL 410

KEY

Upkeep release point **X**

RAF NO 617 SQUADRON LANCASTERS

AJ-L piloted by Flt Lt D. J. Shannon attacked at 0139 – unsuccessful

AJ-Z piloted by Sqn Ldr H. E. Maudslay attacked at 0146 – unsuccessful

AJ-N piloted by Plt Off L. G. Knight attacked at 0152 – successful

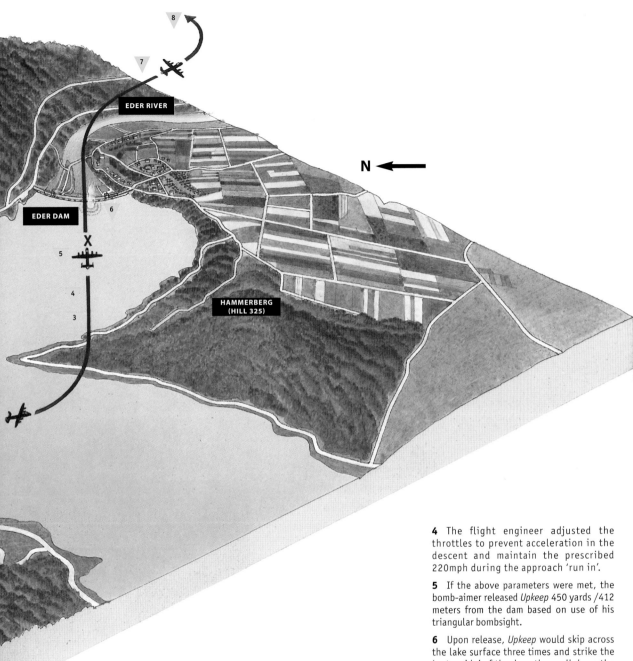

EDER RIVER

EDER DAM

HAMMERBERG
(HILL 325)

N ←

▼ ACTIONS

1 The pilot positioned the aircraft over the narrow valley just west of Waldeck Castle (IP) and initially flew a descending path roughly parallel to the axis of the dam.

2 Approaching the 'run-in' course, the pilot turned left to point at the centre of the dam, flying across a lower slope of the Hammerberg, offset left of the prescribed perpendicular approach course to minimize the amount of descent required.

3 Immediately after crossing the Hammerberg, the pilot descended to and maintained a height of 60 feet above the lake surface cuing off the navigator's 'high'/'low'/'steady' calls based on the two 'altimeter spotlights'.

4 The flight engineer adjusted the throttles to prevent acceleration in the descent and maintain the prescribed 220mph during the approach 'run in'.

5 If the above parameters were met, the bomb-aimer released *Upkeep* 450 yards /412 meters from the dam based on use of his triangular bombsight.

6 Upon release, *Upkeep* would skip across the lake surface three times and strike the 'water side' of the dam, then roll down the dam wall before detonating at 30 foot depth.

7 Upon weapon release – or passing over the dam – the pilot called for maximum power and pulled up sharply to clear the steeply rising terrain of the Michelskopf/Hill 420, banking to the right to fly down the Eder valley as they climbed.

8 Upon clearing Hill 420, the pilot would turn left and orbit back to Waldeck Castle if *Upkeep* had not been released, or to view the results of the attack if it had.

deadly 88mm supplemented by a few captured French M36 75mm guns – and two batteries of quick-firing 37mm light flak guns.

German reports indicate that *Flak-Abt.* 665 had engaged some low-flying intruders at about 2330 (most likely Maudslay's formation) and others about an hour later. Just minutes before 'S-for-Sugar' approached, the 37mm battery near Molenschot, west of the airfield, fired on a passing aircraft – probably Ottley's 'C-for-Charlie'. Some of the spent shells damaged nearby Dutch homes. Then, caught by the battalion searchlight, AJ–S hove into view. These guns opened up again, soon being joined by the 37mm battery at Nerhoven (in the airfield's southeast corner). They caught the Lancaster in a dazzling, shifting web of orange tracer streams.

A Dutch eyewitness reported: 'An aircraft approaches from the west at very low altitude and tries to break through the light flak barrage between Molenschot and Gilze-Rijen … Then a fierce spreading red light becomes visible – the aircraft is on fire and crashes at the airfield amongst the buildings and hangars. A most terrific explosion followed.'

In Brown's aircraft, following about ten miles behind but on course, bomb-aimer Sgt Stefan Oancia, RCAF, also witnessed the tragedy. 'Burpee's Lancaster ahead of us, flew over a German airfield and was hit by ground fire, fuel tanks exploding and a ball of flame rising slowly – stopping, then dropping terminated by a huge ball of flame as it hit the ground and the bomb exploded.'

On the airfield itself members of *Ergänzung*/NJG 2, a 'finishing school' for newly arrived aircrew, also witnessed the dramatic crash of Burpee's bomber. Alerted by the passing of the previous Lancaster (Ottley's), they were gathered in front of their barracks watching for the aircraft's return, since they believed it to be an intruder making several attack passes. When Burpee's aircraft appeared it had already been hit. One German witness said: 'The bomber dropped even lower into the trees through which it tore a great swath before crashing into an empty vehicle garage belonging to the airfield flak section. It burned immediately. Seconds later there was an ear-splitting explosion. The crash site was about a hundred metres [328ft] west of the repair hangar, between it and the command post. The shock wave was so strong that it engulfed the *E*/NJG 2 crews standing about six to seven hundred metres [1,970–2,300ft] away.'

Flak-Abt. 665 recorded the destruction of 'S-for-Sugar' (ED865) at 0200. All seven aboard were killed.

Navigation continued to be difficult as the four remaining Lancasters passed Beek and Rees and tried to give the Ruhr flak defences a wide berth. Complicating their tasks were the calls from 5 Group designating targets for each aircraft.

Initially the 5 Group staff decided to divide up the tertiary targets among the reserve force. The group called up 'O-for-Orange' (F/Sgt W. C. 'Bill' Townsend, flying AJ–O) at 0222 with orders to attack the Ennepe Dam, but received no acknowledgement so repeated the call four minutes later. This time wireless operator F/Sgt George Chalmers acknowledged the order.

Meanwhile, at 0224 the codeword 'Dinghy' ('Eder destroyed; attack Sorpe') was sent to 'F-for-Freddie', with wireless operator Sgt Harry

Hewstone acknowledging a minute later. At 0228, Grantham contacted 'Y-for-York' and sent the same codeword a minute later, although there are also unsubstantiated reports that this aircraft was initially directed to attack the Diemel Dam, then was diverted to the Sorpe.

On the half-hour, 5 Group called up 'C-for-Charlie' and a minute later transmitted 'Gilbert' ('attack last-resort target as detailed'; in this case the target would be the Lister Dam). Wireless operator Sgt Jack Guterman acknowledged. At this stage, it seems someone at Grantham got worried that not enough Lancasters were being directed to attack the Sorpe and at 0232 headquarters countermanded the previous order by sending 'Dinghy' to 'C-for-Charlie' as well.

Attempting to maximise the attack on this target – the last main target remaining – the same message was also sent to 'S-for-Sugar' at 0232, and repeated a minute later. There was of course no acknowledgement from Burpee's aircraft.

Thus, in a period of ten minutes 5 Group had issued five separate orders and one, perhaps two, counter-orders. The overall effect was the belief that HQ was directing four Lancasters to attack the Sorpe and one to the Ennepe. However, one Lancaster had already fallen to German flak and a second one was in its death throes even as these transmissions flashed back and forth.

In the midst of this flurry of W/T communications, on the least-defined portion of the ingress route, Ottley strayed about seven miles (11.8km) south of course, flying parallel to and just north of the Lippe River. This area was defended – in an arc from Dülmen to the Möhnesee – by '*Flakgruppe Dortmund*', which included *Flak-Regiment* 124 (four heavy and two light AA battalions) and a searchlight regiment, *Flakscheinwerfer-Regiment* 146.

Passing Hamm, Ottley apparently climbed as high as 500ft (152m) to allow himself, bomb-aimer F/Sgt Thomas Johnston and navigator Fg Off Jack Barrett to locate the small village of Ahlen, the next turn point. The time was 0232 and Guterman, having just received the 'Dinghy' codeword from 5 Group, spoke up over the intercom saying 'Möhne [sic] gone'. Ottley responded with 'We go to …' At that instant 'C-for-Charlie' was suddenly caught by several searchlights and immediately afterwards was devastated by a withering flak barrage. In the rear turret, gunner Sgt Fred Tees felt the impact of repeated hits and saw flames streaming back from the number-two (port-inner) Merlin. Ottley said, 'I'm sorry boys, we've had it …'

From 'F-for-Freddie', Brown and Oancia witnessed their flight leader's destruction. According to Brown, 'Ottley was on my starboard side at about one o'clock [30° right of the nose] and they hit him. He immediately blew up. His tanks went first and then his bomb … the whole valley was just one orange ball.' Oancia explained: 'Ahead and to starboard searchlights broke out and an aircraft was coned at something over a hundred feet; more searchlights and lots of flak and a terrific explosion in the sky. It was one of ours; probably a little too close to Hamm, a heavily defended rail centre, and too high.'

Local residents remembered the big, crippled Lancaster overflying the small village of Hövel (2 miles/3km north of the Lippe, northwest of Hamm)

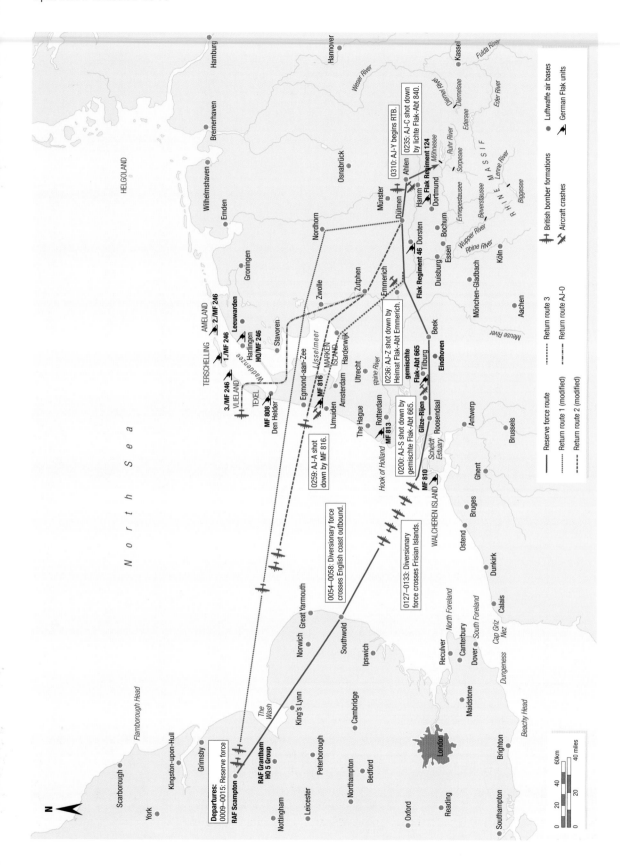

Departures:
0009–0015: Reserve force

RAF Scampton

RAF Grantham
HQ 5 Group

0054–0058: Diversionary force
crosses English coast outbound.

0127–0133: Diversionary
force crosses Frisian Islands.

0200: AJ-S shot down by
gemischte Flak-Abt 665.

0259: AJ-A shot
down by MF 816.

0236: AJ-Z shot down by
Heimat Flak-Abt Emmerich.

0235: AJ-C shot down
by lichte Flak-Abt 840.

0310: AJ-Y begins RTB.

3./MF 246

MF 808
Den Helder

MF 816

MF 813

MF 810

gemischte
Flak-Abt 665
Tilburg

Gilze-Rijen

Flak Regiment 124

Flak Regiment 46 Dorsten

1./MF 246
Harlingen

2./MF 246
Leeuwarden

HQ/MF 246

2./MF 246

Key:
- Reserve force route
- Return route 1 (modified)
- Return route 2 (modified)
- Return route 3
- Return route AJ-O

- Luftwaffe air bases
- German Flak units
- British bomber formations
- Aircraft crashes

N

North Sea

0   20   40   60km
0   20   40 miles

60

before veering northeast, probably as the port fuel tanks exploded and the port wing folded, to crash (at 0235) along the edge of a wood just north of Kötterberg, about 5½ miles (9km) north of Hamm. The *Upkeep* exploded on impact, flinging the tail section well clear of most of the ensuing conflagration. Six crewmen died in the crash, but Tees the tailgunner miraculously survived. He was pulled, severely burned, from the wreckage and taken prisoner.

At 0250, HQ 5 Group repeated the order to 'C-for-Charlie' to attack the Sorpe. Again there was no acknowledgement.

Reserve force attacks: 0300–0341

With the loss of the two pilot officers and their crews, the leading Lancaster in the reserve force became that of F/Sgt Brown. In an impressive display of skill, Brown not only stayed on course the entire way but also amazed his crew with his low flying, pulling up to clear powerlines and their pylons.

Turning south at Ahlen, Brown's aircraft zoomed over the shattered Möhne Dam, the crew noting the deep breach between the towers and the fact that the last surviving 20mm flak gun was still lashing out at the attackers. Angling to the south-southwest, Brown crossed the six miles (9.7km) of darkly wooded and undulating ridges making up the Rhine Massif. Brown reported that by this time, 'All low-lying areas were covered with a fog or mist leaving only the tops of the hills exposed and thus making a determination of the exact ground location impossible.' Circling around, the crew finally identified the Sorpesee and found the dam, nestled silently between the two steep hills.

First taking his position over the Langscheid church spire, Brown then dived down at the dam at a more oblique angle and shot past the target on his first approach. As he later reported: 'I didn't do too well. I got behind [on the "airside" of] the dam on the first run. When I found myself at ground level, behind the dam, I had to climb up roughly 1,800 feet [550m]. It didn't do my nerves any good at all.' Pulling up abruptly, Brown cleared the steep ridge ahead and banked left to circle around and try it again.

The second try went no better and after the third, as Brown swung round to the left in a fairly steep bank, the Lancaster slipped into a descent, settling into the fog that filled the adjacent Röhr River valley before Brown righted the big bomber and pulled up out of the mist. After that Brown had Hewstone drop flares at various points around the circuit to prevent further disorientation.

Finally, on the sixth try, Brown achieved satisfactory parameters and at 0314 Oancia released the *Upkeep*, without backspin, from a height of 60ft (18.3m) just past the midpoint of the dam, on the water side. The depth charge dropped into the water near the dam and disappeared. The Lancaster, with its load released, responded much more nimbly as Brown pulled up to clear the far hill and then banked hard left to get a view. 'After what seemed like ages,' Oancia reported, a large geyser of water erupted near the dam, rising high into the air and falling back slowly into the lake.

MAY 16 1943

2139–2159 Main force departs RAF Scampton

MAY 16 1943

0003–0049 Main force attacks Möhne Dam

The aircraft circled around for a closer look, and the crew observed some 'crumbling' of the crest. At 0323 Hewstone sent the signal 'Goner 78C', indicating that *Upkeep* had been released and exploded in contact with the Sorpe Dam with no apparent breach.

A couple of minutes behind 'F-for-Freddie', F/Sgt Bill Townsend piloted 'O-for-Orange' across the Möhne Valley and angled southwest for 30 miles (48km) towards the Ennepe Dam. This convex masonry dam, built in 1902–4, held back some 12.6 million cubic metres of drinking water and was the only other target directly affecting the Ruhr basin. The Ennepestausee was a rather small but distinctive L-shaped reservoir oriented to the south then east. The dam had the typical paired sluice towers, in this case 600ft (183m) apart.

However, due to the growing mist Townsend and his navigator, Plt Off Lance Howard, RAAF, were unable to locate the Ennepe. On the DR heading across the mist-filled valleys and darkly wooded ridges, Townsend flew southwest for the required ten minutes then, at about 0330, began to orbit in the hope of locating the target.

What he found instead was the Beverstausee – a small artificial lake from which water flowed south into the Wupper River. There were two main differences between the Bever and the Ennepe: the dam-to-reservoir orientation was almost the complete opposite and there were no sluice towers because the Bever was another earthen berm-type dam. However, according to Chalmers, 'it was the right target as far as we were concerned'.[3]

Townsend flew four approaches before bomb-aimer Sgt Charles Franklin released the *Upkeep*, at 0337. The depth charge bounced twice and sank well short of the dam. Thirty seconds later 'a mass of white water shot into the air: it settled, and we saw the dam wall intact'. Townsend circled several times, then – with dawn now rapidly approaching – headed back towards the Möhne to begin the RTB. At 0411 Chalmers sent the signal 'Goner 58E', signifying that the *Upkeep* had been released and exploded 50yd from the Ennepe Dam with no apparent breach.

This was the final result report transmitted because by this time the last Lancaster in the reserve force had already turned for home. Flying 'Y-for-York', F/Sgt Cyril Anderson was off course and behind schedule somewhere around Dülmen when wireless operator Sgt William Bickel received and acknowledged 5 Group's order to attack the Sorpe. In the Buchholt-Borken area Anderson had been forced off track by flak and approaching Dülmen searchlights had forced him further afield. Additionally, rear gunner Sgt W. A. Buck's guns ceased functioning.

Heading towards the dark, rising terrain of the massif, Anderson was even more discouraged by the increasing fog and mist filling the valleys ahead. Considering the mission now impossible, at 0310 he turned around and flew back to RAF Scampton by retracing the ingress route.

---

3 While almost all the literature on the Dams Raid persists in the fiction that 'O-for-Orange' attacked the Ennepe, eyewitness reports from the two villages flanking the Bever Dam and the fact that fragments from the *Upkeep* charge found during the Germans' investigation and renovation of the structure provide convincing evidence that the Bever was attacked, unsuccessfully, instead of the intended target.

Return to base: 0200–0615

By the time Anderson turned around and headed home, the first of the Dambusters was on short finals for landing back at Scampton. At that time, aboard 'J-for-Johnny', David Maltby was calling '[airspeed] below 150, gear down … flaps 20 … [rpm] 2400' as he prepared to set his aircraft down once again on the grass at Scampton.

Three return routes had been laid down in the *Chastise* OpOrd, but none was followed exactly. Maltby initially followed route one, flying the reverse course from the Möhne to Ahlen to the lakes near Dülmen, then a long northerly leg across the flat, sparsely populated farmlands of northern Germany to Nordhorn before turning west again. Crossing the neck of the Helder peninsula north of Alkmaar at 0153 (deviating from the specified route by straightening a dogleg across Holland), the return leg for the first Dambuster was uneventful. With two green lights in the landing gear indicator, flaps at 40 (final setting), and throttles at idle, Maltby gingerly returned 'J-for-Johnny' (ED906) to earth at 0311 after what had been, for his crew, a nearly flawless mission.

Eight minutes behind was 'Mick' Martin, who also followed the modified return route one and continued his ultra-low flying all the way home. Rear gunner F/Sgt Thomas Simpson, RAAF, reported: 'On the way back we saw nothing, thank goodness, but by then I think we were flying at less than 50ft [15m]'.

Since 'T-for-Tommy' had only arrived on the day of the mission launch, there were some difficulties with the compass deviation card. Because of the huge ferrous bulk of *Upkeep*, each aircraft required compass checks – known as a 'compass swing' – when loaded and unloaded. However, in the haste to depart only the compass deviation card for the *Upkeep*-loaded state had been located. Once navigator F/Sgt Don MacLean, RCAF, realised that the crew did not have the 'empty' compass deviation data so as to follow a specified return route, McCarthy said: 'Right, we'll go out the same way as we came in.'

After retracing their ingress routing via Rees, north across the IJsselmeer and over Vlieland, 'T-for-Tommy' approached Scampton directly from the east and landed at 0323. Immediately the big bomber began swinging to the right due to the punctured starboard tyre. 'Joe did a wonderful job. He managed to hold that wheel up by applying aileron until we were just about stopped. We just spun round once.'

From the Ederstausee, Maudslay apparently retraced the ingress route as far as Rees. There he may have been intending to pick up return route three: Rees, Harderwijk, across the IJsselmeer, transiting the Netherlands north of Amsterdam and IJmuiden, and thence directly across the North Sea to Scampton.

Just beyond Rees, Maudslay was apparently following the River Rhine (slightly off course to the west), perhaps so as to allow navigator Fg Off Robert Urquhart, RCAF, to get his bearings and calculate the proper course to Harderwijk. In any event, at 0235 the aircraft approached the river port of Emmerich-am-Rhein from the southeast. On the east side of town was an oil refinery and a large shipping basin used by the many motorised river barges

**MAY 16
1943**

**0009–0015
Reserve force
departs RAF
Scampton**

transporting petroleum products from the refinery. The basin was defended by four batteries belonging to *Heimat-Flakabteilung Emmerich* ('Emmerich Home Flak Unit') – one each north of the railway line on the north side of the basin, on the east edge of the basin, on the Rhine River lock, and on the basin breakwater. Each battery had three rapid-fire 20mm *Flak* 38s.

One of the gunners later reported: 'The aircraft returned from the Ruhr in the early morning. It was fired upon first by the anti-aircraft battery in the keep [basin] … The 'plane turned away [to the right, or north-northeast] and the rear gunner fired at the battery near the lock. Then all twelve guns were shooting at the 'plane and the engines caught fire. Then it crashed and exploded … The aircraft was flying at such low level that our gunfire cut the tops off the poplar trees standing near the harbour.'

At 0236 Maudslay's aircraft (ED937) crashed in flames about two miles (3.2km) north-northeast of the Emmerich basin. All aboard were killed.

After breaching the Eder – and circling the area to witness the results of and relish in their success – the remaining four aircraft of the main strike force began returning home singly. Shannon returned via the modified route one, like Maltby and Martin before him, and after an uneventful flight of more than two hours landed 'L-for-Leather' at Scampton at 0406.

Gibson and Knight turned northwest at the lakes near Dülmen and followed return route two to Zutphen in Holland, then crossed the IJsselmeer so as to cross the Helder peninsula, deviating from the planned track to fly through a known gap in the German flak defences near Egmond-aan-Zee. Shortly before reaching this point Gibson climbed 'G-for-George' for altitude. Then, nosing the big Lancaster – now lighter by 17,000lb (7,711kg) – into a shallow dive, he crossed the coast homebound at about 250mph (402km/hr). Following a peaceful flight across the placid North Sea, he landed 'G-for-George' (ED932) at Scampton at 0415.

Five minutes later Les Knight landed 'N-for-Nuts', having also followed modified route two. Rear gunner Sgt Harry O'Brien, RCAF, reported: 'We were flying very low during the return journey. At the Dutch coast the terrain rose under us.' Knight 'pulled up and down', clearing the piled sand dunes and barely missing a 'large cement block many feet high'. This was most probably a blockhouse – the 66ft (20m) FL250 *Flakgruppenkommandostand* ('group command post and observation tower') built on the dunes near the site of '*Flak-Batterie Dünenberg*', just north of IJmuiden.

Not so lucky were 'Dinghy' Young and his crew aboard 'A-for-Apple'. Young elected to return via route three and after Rees, he steered for Harderwijk, turned 35° left and made a bee-line for the small island of Marken, then apparently followed the Noordhollandskanaal towards IJmuiden, but angled slightly north to avoid the flak concentrations there, hoping to rejoin Gibson's route south of Egmond.

It was accepted practice to climb when approaching the coast (Shannon climbed to 800ft/240m), then dive to gain airspeed (AJ–L reported crossing the shoreline at almost 300mph) and fly through the lethal envelope of coastal flak as quickly as possible. Young may have tried to do this, but was foiled because the Kriegsmarine coastal flak crews had already been alerted by

Gibson's and Knight's high-speed ultra-low overhead flights out to sea – only one minute separates the overflight by AJ–N from the downing of AJ-A.

IJmuiden was defended by *Marine-Flakabteilung* 816, with six heavy, two medium and two light flak batteries; 1. Batterie (four 105mm and two 20mm guns) and 5. *Batterie* (four 88mm and two 20mm guns) were stationed north of the city, along with two small *leichte Flak-Batterien* (two 37mm and three 20mm guns) and the Luftwaffe's l. *Flak-Abt.* 845 (four more 20mm guns).

More than likely, once Knight's 'N-for-Nuts' had blasted past, the observation tower crew looked to the east – against the lightening sky – and saw 'A-for-Apple' climbing, or peaking out at 1,000ft (305m) or so, to begin a 'downhill run' and accelerate out to sea. With the pre-dawn glow behind them and four deadly 88s and a half-dozen *Flak* 38s blazing away 'A-for-Apple' and its crew never had a chance – although Young did apparently try to veer away to the north.

At 0259, near Castricum-aan-Zee (about four miles/7km north of IJmuiden), the stricken 'A-for-Apple' (ED877) smashed into the surf at a shallow angle, almost as if Young was attempting to crash-land headed north, parallel to the beach about 100yd (91.4m) offshore. The Lancaster broke apart at the fuselage joints and all seven crew were killed. The wreckage remained on a sandbar just offshore until 1953 when a vicious storm finally obliterated the remains.

Finally, F/Sgt Brown led the last two Dambusters home, passing over the inundated Möhne valley and through a large amount of air-bursting flak near Hamm before getting properly on course. Turning north at the lakes, Brown followed return route one, and according to flight engineer Sgt Basil Feneron the intrepid NCO pilot 'got down quickly and opened the taps'. Crossing the IJsselmeer, Brown flew at 50ft (15m), using the barometric altimeter because in the early-morning gloom 'there was no horizon – the mud of the Zuider Zee [IJsselmeer] and the sky were all one'.

Making landfall south of the desired track, 'F-for-Freddie' was illuminated by searchlights from both sides and flak opened up ahead. Brown 'put the nose down even lower and piled on maximum boost', but still the air-bursts rocked the big Lancaster, riddling the starboard side with shrapnel and peppering the topside fuselage skin and cockpit canopy. Brown kept his barrelling bomber low, and even in the cockpit some crewmen, such as Feneron, tried to make themselves as small as possible to avoid being hit. Brown crouched behind his instrument panel, flying 'on the gauges' until

The cost: the last of eight Lancasters to be lost that night was that of Sqn Ldr Henry 'Dinghy' Young. AJ–A was shot down during the RTB (return to base). (UK National Archives Photo AIR 20/4367)

MAY 16
1943

0046
AJ–T attacks
Sorpe Dam

they were safely clear. 'F-for-Freddie' (ED918) landed at 0533. After coming to a stop at its hardstand, the exhausted crewmen piled out. The vastly relieved Feneron kissed the earth.

Townsend in 'O-for-Orange' departed the target area a half-hour behind 'F-for-Freddie', so he had the added difficulty of ever-increasing light as the sun began to rise in the east. According to navigator Plt Off Lance Howard, RAAF: 'We turned for the Möhne – found it, and stared amazed at the drop in the water level on the banks of the lake – and still water gushed in a white sheet down the valley.' Leaving the devastation behind, Townsend put the aircraft 'right on the deck' and flew lower than he had ever done before, even during training.

Townsend began the return trip via route two, passing Zutphen, but as the day dawned around them wisely decided to take the course of least inhabitation to get home. After turning west near De Lemmer he flew across the IJsselmeer south of Stavoren, but instead of crossing the Helder peninsula (and possibly experiencing the hot reception 'F-for-Freddie' endured), he turned north to 'sneak between Texel and Vlieland'.

This turn also saved Townsend and his crew from becoming the target of the only interception attempted by a Luftwaffe night-fighter that night. At 0410 – apparently in response to AJ–F flying across the neck of the Helder peninsula south of Alkmaar – *Feldwebels* Kraft and Handke (12./NJG 1) were scrambled once again from *Fliegerhorst* Bergen. Climbing to 6,000m (19,685ft), they patrolled as far south as Zandvoort (*Zone Zander*), reportedly looking for another bomber trailing about a half-hour behind the first. Fortunately, Townsend turned AJ–O to the north just in time. As Handke (who was eventually credited with 59 partnered victories) later lamented: 'The fact that the last aircraft was at low level and had changed its course from west to north-west probably saved it from being shot down.'

Indeed, if 'O-for-Orange' had been spotted from above – racing across the flat Dutch polders in the early morning sunshine – Kraft and Handke's Bf 110G-4a, diving from 19,700ft and developing an 'overtake' of 100mph (160km/h), could have easily caught the lumbering bomber – which had no mid-upper turret – and brought it down with its two Rheinmetall MK108 30mm and two Mauser MG151 20mm cannon.

As AJ–O passed between Texel and Vlieland, *Marine-Flak* 246 opened fire but could not get the correct depression – skipping heavy-calibre rounds off the smooth waters so that the spent shells ricocheted overhead. According to Chalmers: 'The fact that we were so low saved our bacon' (again).

Once safely out to sea the crew could relax somewhat, although the tension returned when flight engineer Sgt Dennis Powell had to shut down one Merlin due to an oil problem. With the crew totally exhausted and squinting in the blazing morning sun, and with only three engines operating, 'O-for-Orange' (ED886) bounced several times before 'sticking' to the earth. Townsend finally called 'flaps up' to kill the lift generated by the wings and gently pulled back on the yoke to lower the tailwheel to the ground so he could begin applying the brakes. The time was 0615. Operation *Chastise* was over, with the mission accomplished.

MAY 16
1943

0130–0152
Main force attacks
Eder Dam

ANALYSIS

'Please tell the special Lancaster unit of my intense admiration for their brilliant operations against the German reservoirs last night.'
Air Chief Marshal Sir Charles Portal, RAF Chief of Staff, to Air Chief Marshal Sir Arthur Harris, AOC-in-C Bomber Command, 17 May 1943.

Chastise was a wartime military operation like many, many others, conceived in the unimaginable urgency of war, executed with determination and courage in the stress of combat, but also subject to the understandable faults and foibles of individuals. None of the negative aspects should be allowed to detract from the courage shown. Making the men's exploits into myth, which many would argue has happened, actually cheapens rather than enhances the Dambusters' accomplishments.

Evaluating these objectively requires them to be compared against the stated aims of the mission on the tactical, operational and strategic levels.

At the tactical level

The stated aims of Operation *Chastise* at its most basic level were to interrupt steel and armaments production in the Ruhr by, in order of importance: flooding factories, damaging transportation infrastructures, disrupting water supply and halting generation of hydro-electric power. No 617 Squadron certainly accomplished this aim, at least temporarily.

The two direct hits on the Möhne-Talsperre resulted in a breach 250ft (76m) wide and 292ft (22m) deep, releasing some 116 cubic metres of water into the Möhne and Ruhr rivers. A torrent 32.8ft (10m) high and travelling at 15 mph (24km/h) swept through the valleys, destroying 11 small factories and 92 homes and damaging another 114 factories and 971 houses along the river. However, these factories did not constitute major steel or armaments concerns: one iron foundry and an aluminium factory were wrecked, but others making artillery shells, small-arms ammunition, aircraft and U-boat parts, and rebar (bunker reinforcement materials) were little harmed.

The transportation network was affected, with 25 road and railway bridges destroyed and another 21 railway bridges damaged along 31 miles

**MAY 16
1943**

**0314
AJ–F attacks
Sorpe Dam**

(50km) of river. River barge traffic was interrupted until the river and its connecting canals could be returned to normal levels about a month later.

The Ruhr industries experienced an immediate though short-lived water shortage due to the clogging of pumping stations with silt and debris from the deluge. Water supplies initially fell to 20% of normal – forcing a 50–60% reduction in the operations of the vital coking plants – but returned to 80% within three days. This is because the industries – and inhabitants' domestic use – primarily drew upon the underground aquifer and local rivers rather than reservoirs. The reservoirs were used to 'backfill' the aquifer during droughts and dry seasons, thus maintaining adequate quantities underground. Adequate rainfall ensured that this did not become a concern in 1943 or 1944.

While the British believed the devastation wrought by the deluge to have had a significant effect, it was actually the loss of hydro-electric power that had the greatest impact on Ruhr armaments production. Two powerplants (producing 5,100kW) associated with the dam were destroyed and seven others were damaged; especially important was the Herdecke plant (132,000kW), where electricity generation was halted for two weeks. However, this represented only 15% of the region's electrical generation capacity and Germany's efficient grid system enabled alternative supplies of electricity to be sourced from as far away as the Alps. Armaments production resumed – at 50% output – on 22 May, returning to full capacity a week later.

Estimates of *Chastise*'s impact on Nazi armaments industries in terms of reductions in productivity vary from 5% to 35%. In truth, the real extent of disruption to production due to this single operation are lost amidst the overall effects of Harris' ongoing Battle of the Ruhr; they cannot be determined separately.

Finally, the official death toll came to 1,294 persons, less than half of whom were German. Sadly, 493 of the dead were Ukrainian women conscript labourers, drowned in their camp barracks. *Chastise* caused the greatest loss of life of any single RAF attack thus far in the war.

The destruction of the Eder had a similar though smaller effect, with much less strategic impact. Knight's direct hit caused a breach 230ft (70m) wide and 292ft (22m) deep, releasing some 154 cubic metres of water. Four power stations (all associated with the dam) were put out of action, 14 bridges were destroyed, some 101 'workplaces' – none of them having anything to do with the war effort – affected, and 47 people killed.

At the operational level

At the operational or 'campaign' level the aim was to spread panic among the population and lower the enemy's morale, while boosting morale on the British home front with a dramatic and decisive exploit.

The former objective proved difficult to achieve, especially against a nationalistic police state such as Adolf Hitler's Nazi Germany. There were a few random reports – such as the 18 May *New York Times*/Reuters 'telegram from Berne' – claiming that the German public had become apprehensive about Allied air attacks because they could cause floods, and claiming that civil unrest had developed in affected areas due to the flooding. However, there was no measurable evidence that this aim had been met.

On the other hand, there was a tremendous uplift for the British populace. Coming as it did on the heels of the final Allied victory in North Africa – announced on 13 May – the mission's success had 'a great psychological effect on people's morale', especially considering it was solely a British undertaking.

The PR blitz began shortly after the last Dambuster landed, with the first Air Ministry communiqué being enthusiastically broadcast by the BBC. The story – fed by follow-up official statements emphasising the raid's spectacular results – was front-page news in the London and provincial papers that evening. Next morning the first RAF photo-reconnaissance pictures were released, adding fuel to the spreading media wildfire. On 18 May the *Daily Mail* ran a major story headlined 'The smash-up: RAF picture testifies to perfect bombing'. The media extravaganza climaxed on 22 and 29 May with two-page spreads in the *Illustrated London News*, one of them headlined 'A titanic

blow at Germany: RAF smash Europe's mightiest dams'. From all this, the legend was born. Many of the myths it generated persist today.

Because of the 'most secret' nature of the *Upkeep* weapon and its employment (the bomb was not declassified until 1962), the official PR campaign necessarily included significant misinformation aimed at misleading the enemy. It also succeeded in misleading subsequent historians. The most significant misinformation related to AJ–O's attack on the Ennepe/Bever dam. In post-strike documentation and public information releases – including the official report to the War Cabinet by Secretary of State for Air Sir Archibald Sinclair – it is stated that F/Sgt Townsend and his crew attacked the 'Schwelme Dam'. Schwelme is a town lying partway between the Ennepe and Bever and has no lake or dam of its own. By claiming that O-for-Orange's attack was against this (fictitious) dam, and associating the correct target with a location close to the actual attack, the Air Ministry concealed the fact that the wrong target was hit. That this is a post-strike fabrication is evidenced by the fact that the descriptor 'Schwelme Dam' does not occur in any of the mission planning documentation. Interestingly, Townsend's crew received more awards than any other crew involved in the Dams Raid except Gibson's.

At the strategic level

It was at the highest level that the British obtained the greatest benefit from the exploits of and sacrifices by these 133 men, who delivered 11 *Upkeep* weapons against four German dams and successfully breached two of them.

This RAF next-day post-strike reconnaissance photo shows the limited damage to the crest of the Sorpe Dam and the wash of water staining the airside of the dam as it flowed into and muddied the holding reservoir. This effect resulted from splash overflow after McCarthy's and Brown's weapons detonated in the water near the dam. (UK National Archives Photo AIR 34/609)

At the time of the raid Winston Churchill and the British chiefs of staff were in Washington DC attending the 15-day 'Trident' US–UK–Canada summit conference, reviewing plans and priorities for implementing the Casablanca decisions on the Allied bombing campaign against Germany, the invasion of Italy and planned Pacific campaigns. The British had been confronted by American scepticism over British leadership, military capabilities and priorities. The timely announcement of *Chastise*'s success immediately and dramatically demonstrated British technical expertise as well as a moral ascendancy over the mutual enemy.

The Americans, still outraged at the Japanese 'sneak attack' on Pearl Harbor, wanted to concentrate US air and naval strength against Japan, at the cost of the combined air offensive against Germany and the campaign against U-boats in the Atlantic. They also wanted to use available amphibious shipping – which at this stage was limited – against Japanese-held islands which could be used as airbases, rather than against Sicily and mainland Italy. *Chastise*'s success helped Churchill to win over his larger ally to the 'Germany-first' and Mediterranean strategies.

Another effect, though not as immediately visible, was on the Soviet Union. Stalin and the Soviet military leadership were suitably impressed. In March Churchill had curtailed Arctic supply convoys so as to be able to amass shipping for the invasion of Sicily; in compensation, he had promised Stalin more effective bombing of Germany. *Chastise*'s success certainly appeared to fulfil this promise. On 18 May Stalin signalled his congratulations to Churchill in Washington.

The final analysis

In an amazing feat of arms – even without its elevation to legend – the crews of 617 Sqn successfully conducted a dramatic and effective strike against the Third Reich. Of the three main targets specified by the Air Ministry (strategic-level HQ), the first and third were destroyed. The second main target (and the secondary target at the tactical level, in terms of mission planning by HQ 5 Group and 617 Sqn) was unsuccessfully attacked by two *Chastise* bombers.

The lack of success against the Sorpe should not be seen as any kind of failure on the part of the crews. Two *Upkeep* weapons were delivered as close to prescribed parameters as humanly possible. According to German post-strike examination, the bombs exploded within 98ft (30m) of each other, only 9.8ft (3m) beneath the surface and caused some 230ft (70m) of the dam's crown to crumble. However, inspection using the dam's internal maintenance tunnels found no cracks or seepage.

The basic fact was that the earthen berm-type dam was not vulnerable to *Upkeep*, and including the Sorpe on the

Debriefing Gibson's crew. At the table are a 617 Sqn intelligence officer, Spafford, Taerum and Trevor-Roper; Pulford and Deering are out of shot to the right. ACM Sir Arthur Harris and AVM The Hon. R. A. Cochrane look on. It is a strong measure of the RAF's appreciation of this event from a propaganda perspective that the focus immediately after the mission was almost exclusively on Gibson and his crew. (IWM Photo CH 9683)

target list using this weapon was an erroneous operational decision. AVM Bottomley's original 18 March assessment in this regard was correct and Wallis' assurances that *Upkeep* could work against Sorpe were unjustified. In modern times this would be known as a 'weaponeering error', for which the planning staff bear full responsibility.

A second operational error was not including the Sorpe in the mission briefing for the reserve-force aircrews. They were briefed to attack targets 'A' and 'B', if these still stood, or individually assigned 'targets of last resort' based on W/T orders from 5 Group. To expect the crews to successfully attack a target for which they were not briefed is clearly inappropriate. The fact that HQ 5 Group developed the OpOrd excluding the Sorpe from the reserve force's target list, then changed assignments 'on the fly' to include that dam, clearly demonstrates where the fault lay.

This fact makes more understandable F/Sgt Cyril Anderson's decision to abort the mission when mounting adversity clearly compromised any hopes of success. However, Gibson did not see it that way. Allowing his prejudice against NCOs to take full rein, he furiously accused the crew of simply having 'flown up and down the North Sea the full time'. Following the obligatory PR photos, Anderson and his crew were returned to 49 Sqn. Four months later they were lost during a raid on Mannheim. They are buried together in Rheinberg Cemetery, very close to the graves of 617 Sqn comrades John Hopgood and four of his crewmen.

For his part, Gibson soon handed over the 'Dambusters Squadron' to Sqn Ldr George Holden and on 4 August departed with Winston Churchill's party for Quebec, Canada, and the 'Quadrant' conference. After a week of official and social duties, Gibson went on a five-week nationwide tour of RCAF bases in a rousingly popular morale and PR tour. This was followed by a six-week coast-to-coast tour of major US cities, giving more than 150 speeches and radio interviews.

When Gibson returned to Britain he was sidelined in the Air Ministry – the Directorate of Accidents – ostensibly to supervise the writing of his wartime memoir, *Enemy Coast Ahead*. However, he also used this time to parlay his VC into a potential Parliamentary seat (although he eventually came to regret this and withdrew).

Finally, in August 1944 Gibson returned to operations, with a posting as SASO to HQ No 54 Base at RAF Coningsby, home of 5 Group's 'master-bomber' force. The force comprised a collection of experienced pilots and observers gathered into 83 Sqn, 97 Sqn and 627 Sqn that were responsible for tactical control of bombing operations. Gibson had flown several familiarisation sorties as a passenger on these missions and eventually was permitted to lead one himself.

On 19 November 1944, flying 627 Sqn Mosquito AZ–E (KB267) with 23-year-old Acting Sqn Ldr Jim Warwick, he directed a 200-bomber mission against railyards at Mönchengladbach and Reydt. However, when the aircraft began its RTB its Merlins failed – probably due to fuel starvation, since neither man was familiar with the Mosquito's fuel transfer procedures – and the aircraft crashed near Steenbergen, Holland, killing both men.

**MAY 16
1943**

**0337
AJ–O attacks
Bever Dam**

**MAY 16
1943**

**0311–0615
Surviving aircraft
land at RAF
Scampton**

CONCLUSION

'We have made attempt after attempt to pull successful low [altitude] attacks with heavy bombers. They have been, almost without exception, costly failures…'

Air Chief Marshal Sir Arthur Harris, in a personal letter to Air Chief Marshal Sir Charles Portal, attempting to dissuade him from ordering Operation *Chastise*, 18 February 1943.

Despite Harris' discouraging warning, 19 Lancasters were despatched to destroy at least three strategic dams supplying water and electrical power to the German armaments industry in the Ruhr. Three of these aircraft, for various reasons, had to abort the mission. Sixteen continued to the target area.

Of the 16 Lancasters that were able to press on, six were assigned to attack the Möhne, and following its breaching three more aircraft attacked the Eder. The two primary targets were destroyed. However, one of the attacking bombers was lost *en route*, another during the attack and two

Maximising PR potential, AVM Cochrane, Gibson, RAF Scampton commander Gp Cpt J. N. H. Whitworth and another officer (to the right) explain the Dams Raid to King George VI using the Möhne Dam briefing model at Scampton, during the royal visit of 27 May 1943. (IWM Photo CH 9924)

more were lost during egress – so accomplishing the mission cost four out of nine assigned aircraft.

Of the other seven Lancasters, six – three each from the diversionary and reserve forces – were assigned to attack the Sorpe, the secondary target, and the seventh to attack the Ennepe, the only tertiary target affecting the Ruhr basin. Of the six aircraft sent against the Sorpe, four were lost on ingress, so only two bombers made ineffectual attacks on that dam. Due to insurmountable difficulties the aircraft assigned to the Ennepe was unable to locate its target and executed an ineffective attack against an entirely different dam.

Operation *Chastise* can best be assessed overall as a successful strike but, as ACM Harris warned, the cost was prohibitively high: 50% of the attacking force was lost in the raid. In fact, the next major mission of 617 Sqn saw the loss of two more original Dambuster crews.

The unit moved to RAF Coningsby on 30 August 1943, and after flying three missions dropping bombs and leaflets on Italian targets, set off to breach the levées of the Dortmund–Ems Canal – with the aim of flooding the immediate area and halting barge traffic on this and adjacent waterways – using Wallis' new 12,000lb high-capacity 'Blockbuster' bombs.

Sqn Ldr David Maltby – the pilot of the aircraft whose bomb finally breached the Möhne – and his crew were all killed during the mission. In the midst of crossing the North Sea at minimum height, the attack was scrubbed by 5 Group. Maltby's Lancaster caught a wingtip in the water (most probably during the low-altitude turn to RTB) and cartwheeled into the sea. The raid was resumed the next night, and during the attack Sqn Ldr George Holden and most of AJ–G's original crew were lost; so was Flt Lt Les Knight, although he did manage to maintain control of his stricken Lancaster so his crew could successfully bale out. The target was not even dented, and no further ultra-low bombing missions were ever flown.

Throughout 1943 and early 1944 there were discussions about how the remaining 40 *Upkeep* weapons might be used (centring on possible land targets), but in the event the bombs were placed in storage at Scampton. The ten surviving 'Dambuster' Lancasters – out of the original 23 Type 464 Provisioning B.IIIs – were also placed in storage, at RAF Lossiemouth. In early 1947 three of these were returned to airworthy status, had their *Upkeep*-specific gear re-mounted and were sent to Scampton. Between 22 August and 21 December the weapons were dropped into the North Sea from 10,000ft, without being armed.

This disposal of the unique weapons – and the eventual scrapping of the last Type 464 Lancasters – brought an end to the story of this amazing, and now iconic, British military experience.

For the rest of the war 617 Sqn held pride of place as an elite RAF unit, its Lancasters and crews going on to gain further fame in raids using the 'Grand Slam' earthquake bomb (shown here) and on the *Tirpitz*. Today, the squadron remains on the RAF's order of battle, just as its legendary 'Dambusters Raid' remains part of the consciousness of British people generations removed from the event. (IWM Photo MH 4263)

BIBLIOGRAPHY

For the serious student of Operation *Chastise*, the books, magazine articles and websites listed below are recommended.

Arthur, Max, *Dambusters: A Landmark Oral History* (Virgin Books: London, 2008).

Bateman, Alex, *Aviation Elite Units 34: No 617 'Dambuster' Sqn* (Osprey Publishing: Oxford, 2009).

Brown, Ken, 'Ken Brown CGM: Dam buster' *Bomber Command Museum of Canada* (Bomber Command Museum of Canada: Nanton, Canada, 1993). Website, available online at:
www.bombercommandmuseum.ca/kenbrown.html

Cooper, Alan, *The Men Who Breached the Dams* (Airlife Publishing: Shrewsbury, 2002).

Cotter, Jarrod, 'Avro Lancaster', *Aviation Classics*, No. 1, November 2009.

Dambusters 2010 *Dambusters* website, available at:
www.dambusters.org.uk

Euler, Helmuth, *The Dams Raid Through the Lens* (After the Battle: Old Harlow, 2001).

Foster, Charles, *Breaking the Dams: The Story of Dambuster David Maltby and His Crew* (Pen & Sword Books: Barnsley, 2008).

Fraser, John 'John Fraser & "Hoppy"', *Bomber Command Museum of Canada* (Bomber Command Museum of Canada: Nanton, Canada, 2010). Website, available online at:
www.bombercommandmuseum.ca/fraserhoppy.html

Gibson, Guy, *Enemy Coast Ahead* (Michael Joseph: London, 1953).

Gibson, Guy, *Enemy Coast Ahead*, annotated and illustrated by Chaz Bowyer (Bridge Books: Wrexham, 1995).

McCormac, Mike, 'Re-flying the Dams Raid', *After the Battle*, No. 82, May 1993.

Morris, Richard, *Guy Gibson* (Penguin Books: London, 1995).

Munro, Les, 'A Kiwi with the Dam Busters', *Aviation Classics*, No. 1, November 2009.

National Archives, *Dambusters* (National Archives: Richmond, UK, 2010). Website, available online at: www.nationalarchives.gov.uk/dambusters

Ottaway, Susan, *Dambuster: The Life of Guy Gibson VC, DSO, DFC* (Pen & Sword Books: Barnsley, 2007).

Ramsay, Winston G., 'The Ruhr Dams Raid 1943', *After the Battle*, No. 3, August 1973.

Sweetman, John, *The Dambusters Raid* (Arms & Armour Press, London: 1990).

Thorning, Arthur G., *The Dambuster Who Cracked the Dam* (Pen & Sword Books: Barnsley, 1998).

Ward, Chris, and Andreas Wachtel, *Dambuster Crash Sites: 617 Dambuster Squadron Crash Sites in Holland and Germany* (Pen & Sword Books: Barnsley, 2007).

Ward, Chris, Andy Lee and Andreas Wachtel, *Dambusters: The Definitive History of 617 Squadron at War 1943–1945* (Red Kite: Walton-on-Thames, 2008).

Ward, Chris and Andy Lee, *Images of War: 617 Dambusters Squadron at War* (Pen & Sword Books: Barnsley, 2009).

Extending the enthusiastic publicity attending the successful Dambusters Raid, Sqn Ldr David J. Maltby, DSO, DFC, and Acting Wg Cdr Guy P. Gibson, VC, DSO, DFC, were photographed in July, as they posed in Gibson's Hangar 2 second-floor corner office (note fake window scenery), ostensibly reviewing magazines publicising their dramatic exploits. (IWM Photo TR 1122)

APPENDIX

No 617 Squadron crews of the main strike force ('Wave One')

Position	Rank, name, service (if not RAF)	Prior awards	*Chastise* awards	Fate during World War II
Lancaster AJ–G (ED932)			Attacked Möhne Dam; ineffective	
Pilot	Acting Wg Cdr Guy Gibson	DSO and Bar; DFC and Bar	VC	KIA, 19–20 September 1944
Navigator	Plt Off H. T. Taerum, RCAF		DFC	KIA, 15–16 September 1943
Bomb-aimer	Plt Off F. M. Spafford, RAAF	DFM	DFC	As above
Wireless operator	Flt Lt R. E. G. Hutchison	DFC	Bar	As above
Flight engineer	Sgt J. Pulford		DFM	DIA, 13 February 1944
Front gunner	F/Sgt G. A. Deering, RCAF		DFC	KIA, 15–16 September 1943
Rear gunner	Flt Lt R. D. Trevor-Roper	DFM	DFC	KIA, 30–31 March 1944
Lancaster AJ–M (ED925)			Lost; shot down by flak over Möhne Dam	
Pilot	Flt Lt J. V. Hopgood	DFC and Bar		KIA, Dams Raid, 16–17 May 1943
Navigator	Fg Off P. S. Earnshaw, RCAF			As above
Bomb-aimer	F/Sgt J. W. Fraser, RCAF			As above
Wireless operator	Sgt J. W. Minchin			As above
Flight engineer	Sgt C. Brennan			As above
Front gunner	Plt Off G. H. F. G. Gregory	DFM		As above
Rear gunner	Plt Off A. F. Burcher, RAAF	DFM		As above
Lancaster AJ–P (ED909)			Attacked Möhne Dam; ineffective	
Pilot	Flt Lt H. B. Martin	DFC	DSO	
Navigator	Flt Lt J. F. Leggo, RAAF	DFC	Bar	
Bomb-aimer	Flt Lt R. C. Hay, RAAF	DFC	Bar	KIA, 12–13 February 1944
Wireless operator	Fg Off L. Chambers, RNZAF		DFM	
Flight engineer	Plt Off I. Whittaker			
Front Gunner	Plt Off B. T. Foxlee, RAAF	DFM		
Rear Gunner	F/Sgt T. D. Simpson, RAAF		DFM	
Lancaster AJ–A (ED877)			Lost; shot down by flak near IJmuiden	
Pilot	Sqn Ldr H. M. Young	DFC and Bar		KIA, Dams Raid, 16–17 May 1943
Navigator	F/Sgt C. W. Roberts			As above
Bomb-aimer	Fg Off V. S. MacCausland, RCAF			As above
Wireless operator	Sgt L. W. Nichols			As above
Flight engineer	Sgt D. T. Horsfall			As above
Front gunner	Sgt G. A. Yeo			As above
Rear gunner	Sgt W. Ibbotson			As above

No 617 Squadron crews of the main strike force ('Wave One') *continued*

Position	Rank, name, service (if not RAF)	Prior awards	*Chastise* awards	Fate during World War II
Lancaster AJ–J (ED906)			Attacked Möhne Dam; effective	
Pilot	Flt Lt D. J. H. Maltby	DFC	DSO	KIA, 14–15 September 1943
Navigator	Sgt V. Nicholson		DFM	As above
Bomb-aimer	Plt Off J. Fort		DFC	As above
Wireless operator	Sgt A. J. B. Stone			As above
Flight engineer	Sgt W. Hatton			As above
Front gunner	Sgt V. Hill			As above
Rear gunner	Sgt H. T. Simmonds			As above
Lancaster AJ–L (ED929)			Attacked Eder Dam; ineffective	
Pilot	Flt Lt D. J. Shannon, RAAF	DFC	DSO	
Navigator	Fg Off D. R. Walker, RCAF	DFC	Bar	
Bomb-aimer	F–Sgt L. J. Sumpter		DFM	
Wireless operator	Fg Off B. Goodale	DFC		
Flight engineer	Sgt R. J. Henderson			
Front Gunner	Sgt B. Jagger			
Rear Gunner	Fg Off J. Buckley		DFC	DIA, 30 April 1944
Lancaster AJ–Z (ED937)			Lost; shot down by flak near Emmerich	
Pilot	Sqn Ldr H. E. Maudslay	DFC		KIA, Dams Raid, 16–17 May 1943
Navigator	Fg Off R. A. Urquhart, RCAF	DFC		As above
Bomb-aimer	Plt Off M. J. D. Fuller			As above
Wireless operator	WO A. P. Cottam			As above
Flight engineer	Sgt G. Marriott	DFM		As above
Front gunner	Fg Off W. J. Tytherleigh	DFC		As above
Rear gunner	Sgt N. R. Burrows			As above
Lancaster AJ–B (ED864)			Lost; collided with electricity pylon	
Pilot	Flt Lt W. Astell	DFC		KIA, Dams Raid, 16–17 May 1943
Navigator	Plt Off F. A. Wile, RCAF			As above
Bomb-aimer	Fg Off D. Hopkinson			As above
Wireless operator	WO A. A. Garshowitz, RCAF			As above
Flight engineer	Sgt J. Kinnear			As above
Front gunner	F/Sgt F. A. Garbas, RCAF			As above
Rear gunner	Sgt R. Bolitho			As above
Lancaster AJ–N (ED912)			Attacked Eder Dam; effective	
Pilot	Plt Off L. G. Knight, RAAF		DSO	KIA, 15–16 September 1943
Navigator	Fg Off H. S. Hobday		DFC	
Bomb-aimer	Fg Off E. C. Johnson		DFC	
Wireless operator	F/Sgt R. G. T. Kellow, RAAF			
Flight engineer	Sgt R. E. Grayston			POW, 15–16 September 1943
Front gunner	Sgt F. E. Sutherland, RCAF			
Rear gunner	Sgt H. C. O'Brien			POW, 15–16 September 1943

617 Squadron crews of the diversionary force ('Wave Two')

Position	Rank, name, service (if not RAF)	Prior awards	*Chastise* awards	Fate during World War II
Lancaster AJ–T (ED825)			Attacked Sorpe Dam; ineffective	
Pilot	Flt Lt J. C. McCarthy, RCAF	DFC	DSO	
Navigator	Fg Off D. A. MacClean, RCAF		DFM	
Bomb-aimer	Sgt G. L. Johnson		DFM	
Wireless operator	F/Sgt L. Eaton			
Flight engineer	Sgt W. G. Radcliff, RCAF			
Front gunner	Sgt R. Batson			
Rear gunner	Fg Off D. Rodger, RCAF			
Lancaster AJ–E (ED927)			Lost when collided with electricity pylon	
Pilot	Flt Lt R. N. G. Barlow, RAAF	DFC		KIA, Dams Raid, 16–17 May 1943
Navigator	Fg Off P. S. Burgess			As above
Bomb–aimer	Plt Off A. Gillespie	DFM		As above
Wireless operator	Fg Off C. R. Williams, RAAF	DFC		As above
Flight engineer	Plt Off S. L. Whillis			As above
Front gunner	Fg Off H. S. Glinz, RCAF			As above
Rear gunner	Sgt J. R. G. Liddell			As above
Lancaster AJ–W (ED921)			RTB early; damaged by flak	
Pilot	Flt Lt J. L. Munro, RNZAF			
Navigator	Fg Off F. G. Rumbles			
Bomb-aimer	Sgt J. H. Clay			
Wireless operator	WO P. E. Pigeon, RCAF			
Flight engineer	Sgt F. E. Appleby			
Front gunner	Sgt W. Howarth			
Rear gunner	F/Sgt H. A. Weeks, RCAF			
Lancaster AJ–K (ED934)			Lost; shot down by flak over Waddenzee	
Pilot	Plt Off V. W. Byers, RCAF			KIA, Dams Raid, 16–17 May 1943
Navigator	Fg Off J. H. Warner			As above
Bomb-aimer	Plt Off A. N. Whittaker			As above
Wireless operator	Sgt J. Wilkinson			As above
Flight engineer	Sgt A. J. Taylor			As above
Front gunner	Sgt C. McA. Jarvie			As above
Rear gunner	F/Sgt J. McDowell, RCAF			As above
Lancaster AJ–H (ED836)			RTB early; *Upkeep* lost in collision with sea	
Pilot	Plt Off G. Rice			POW, 20–21 December 1943
Navigator	Fg Off R. MacFarlane			As above
Bomb-aimer	WO J. W. Thrasher, RCAF			As above
Wireless operator	WO C. B. Gowrie, RCAF			As above
Flight engineer	Sgt E. C. Smith			As above
Front gunner	Sgt T. W. Maynard			As above
Rear gunner	Sgt S. Burns			As above

No 617 Squadron crews of the reserve force ('Wave Three')

Position	Rank, name, service (if not RAF)	Prior awards	*Chastise* awards	Fate during World War II
Lancaster AJ–C (ED910)			Lost; shot down by flak over Hamm	
Pilot	Plt Off W. H. T. Ottley	DFC		KIA, Dams Raid, 16–17 May 1943
Navigator	Fg Off J. K. Barrett	DFC		As above
Bomb-aimer	F/Sgt T. B. Johnston			As above
Wireless operator	Sgt J. Guterman	DFM		As above
Flight engineer	Sgt R. Marsden			As above
Front gunner	Sgt H. J. Strange			As above
Rear gunner	Fg Off F. Tees			As above
Lancaster AJ–S (ED865)			Lost; shot down by flak over Gilze Rijen	
Pilot	Plt Off L. J. Burpee, RCAF	DFM		KIA, Dams Raid, 16–17 May 1943
Navigator	Sgt T. Jaye			As above
Bomb-aimer	F/Sgt J. L. Arthur, RCAF			As above
Wireless operator	Plt Off L. G. Weller	DFC		As above
Flight engineer	Sgt G. Pegler			As above
Front gunner	Sgt W. C. A. Long			As above
Rear gunner	WO J. G. Brady, RCAF			As above
Lancaster AJ–F (ED918)			Attacked Sorpe Dam; ineffective	
Pilot	F/Sgt K. W. Brown, RCAF		CGM	
Navigator	Sgt D. P. Heal		DFM	
Bomb-aimer	Sgt S. Oancia, RCAF		DFM	KIA, 12–13 February 1944
Wireless operator	Sgt H. J. Hewstone			
Flight engineer	Sgt H. B. Feneron			
Front gunner	Sgt D. Allatson			
Rear gunner	F/Sgt G. S. MacDonald, RCAF			
Lancaster AJ–O (ED886)			Attacked Bever Dam; ineffective	
Pilot	F/Sgt W. C. Townsend	DFM	CGM	KIA, Dams Raid, 16–17 May 1943
Navigator	Plt Off C. L. Howard, RAAF		DFC	As above
Bomb-aimer	Sgt C. E. Franklin	DFM	Bar	As above
Wireless operator	F/Sgt G. A. Chalmers		DFM	As above
Flight engineer	Sgt D. J. D. Powell			As above
Front gunner	Sgt D. E. Webb		DFM	As above
Rear gunner	Sgt R. Wilkinson,		DFM	As above
Lancaster AJ–Y (ED924)			RTB early; conditions precluded success	
Pilot	F/Sgt C. T. Anderson		DSO	KIA, 14–15 September 1943
Navigator	Sgt J. P. Nugent		DFM	As above
Bomb-aimer	Sgt G. J. Green		DFC	As above
Wireless operator	Sgt W. D. Bickle			As above
Flight engineer	Sgt R. C. Paterson			
Front gunner	Sgt E. Ewan			
Rear gunner	Sgt A. W. Buck			

INDEX

Figures in **bold** refer to illustrations